Lost Black Cats

Story of Two Captured Chinese U-2 Pilots

By

H. Mike Hua

1663 Liberty Drive, Suite 200
Bloomington, Indiana 47403
(800) 839-8640
www.AuthorHouse.com

© 2005 H. Mike Hua. All Rights Reserved.

No part of this book may be reproduced, stored in a retrieval system, or transmitted by any means without the written permission of the author.

First published by AuthorHouse 03/10/05

ISBN: 1-4184-9917-X (sc)
ISBN: 1-4184-9918-8 (dj)

Library of Congress Control Number: 2005901072

Printed in the United States of America
Bloomington, Indiana

This book is printed on acid-free paper.

Table of Contents

Preface vii

Chapter One: Solitary Confinement 1

Chapter Two: Interrogation 15

Chapter Three: Social Unrest 31

Chapter Four: Reeducation 49

Chapter Five: New Hope 74

Chapter Six: Unexpected Promotion 91

Chapter Seven: Permission to Leave the Mainland 107

Chapter Eight: Jack's Miserable Story 122

Chapter Nine: Free at Last? 142

Chapter Ten: Ordeal in Hong Kong 157

Chapter Eleven: American Odyssey 175

Chapter Twelve: Rehabilitation 192

Epilogue 206

Preface

The idea of writing this book arose right after I attended a dinner party held in Taipei, Taiwan, on September 5, 1990. The dinner was hosted by General Lin Wenli, Commander-in-Chief of the Republic of China Air Force (ROCAF), to welcome two Chinese Nationalist ex-U-2 pilots who had been shot down over the China mainland in 1963 and 1965 and who had been permitted to return to Taiwan only a day before. At that time I was Director General of the Aero Industry Development Center, an indigenous aircraft industry in Taiwan, and was under a tight schedule to lead more than two thousand engineers and technicians in developing and producing a state-of-the-art supersonic jet fighter, IDF, for the urgent air defense needs of the Republic of China in Taiwan. As I was one of a few surviving Chinese U-2 pilots, I temporarily released myself from the heavy workload and drove two and half an hours from Taichung to participate in that dinner.

The U-2 was and remains today a most capable spy airplane. When the Russians had developed nuclear weapons of various degrees of sophistication, and followed that with jet bombers flying over Moscow at the May Day air show in 1954, the United States government had grown increasingly concerned over a possible surprise nuclear attack by the Soviet Union. There was no U.S. conventional espionage behind the Iron Curtain able to find out how fast the Russians were producing this bomber and when they could achieve the capability to launch that attack. The countermeasure the Eisenhower administration developed was a high-altitude photoreconnaissance aircraft that could cruise at an altitude no enemy jet interceptors could reach, fly long enough to reach deep inside enemy territory, and carry a camera that could detect enemy activities on the ground. That situation is what gave birth to the U-2.

Under the management of the CIA, the U-2s began penetrating the Soviet Union airspace in 1956. The operations were very successful. The airborne camera could bring back a photo map of roughly two thousand miles in length by one hundred miles in width, which revealed not only the precise location of a target, but also the activities on the ground. The electronics on board the U-2 could also bring back enormous amounts of hostile communications and electromagnetic signals. The intelligence collected was extremely valuable in shaping the strategy of the free world against the Communist bloc.

Unfortunately, one of these missions failed on May 1, 1960. A U-2 piloted by Gary Powers was shot down inside Soviet territory by surface-to-air missiles and the pilot was captured. This incident impacted significantly on the long-awaited Paris Summit Meeting of world leaders scheduled for the 16th of May. In that meeting Premier Khrushchev denounced the U.S. "aggression" and demanded that President Eisenhower make a formal apology. The U-2 had now become a world-renowned spyplane. From that time on, the U-2 was no longer dispatched to penetrate Soviet airspace, but other parts of the world.

With CIA assistance, a US-ROC joint squadron of U-2s, the Black Cat Squadron, was established in Taiwan. Chinese Nationalist pilots started penetrating the airspace over the China mainland and its vicinities in 1962, and continued until 1974.

Years later, on September 17, 1998, the CIA held a public symposium titled "U-2: A Revolution in Intelligence" to declassify most of the CIA-controlled U-2 operations to comply with the requirement of the Freedom of Information Act. In his opening speech, CIA director George J. Tenet said:

"... The U-2 was, indeed, one of the CIA's greatest intelligence achievements. In fact, it may be one of the greatest achievements of any nation...."

The symposium did pay tribute to the participants of the U-2 project who had died in the line of duty, including ten Chinese pilots, but for some reason did not release any information on the US-ROC joint "Black Cat" Squadron. As a matter of fact, this US-ROC joint operation was the longest and most courageous of the entire U-2 history. Comparing to other U-2 operations, American U-2s penetrated the Iron Curtain twenty-four times, with one aircraft shot down by missiles and no pilots sacrificed. The U-2s of the Black Cat Squadron penetrated the Bamboo Curtain one hundred and two times, with five aircraft shot down, three pilots killed, and two captured by the enemy.

These two captured Black Cats, Yeh Changti and Chang Liyi, were severely wounded when the Russian-built surface-to-air missiles destroyed their U-2s. Then they were incarcerated and confined in the mainland for almost nineteen years. They lived through the turbulent years of the notorious Cultural Revolution in the People's Republic of China. Their loving families in Taiwan were ruined completely. By the time these two courageous pilots were allowed to leave Communist China, their loyalty was questioned strongly by their own government in Taiwan.

As an ex-U-2 pilot myself, I had especial sympathy for them. Most of all for Yeh, who had been my roommate for many months in Taiwan when we were both working for the Black Cat Squadron. At that time, I was about to complete my duty (ten overflights) and be released from that squadron, whereas Yeh was the new blood of the operation. Although he was around thirty years old, he was still the youngest pilot in that squadron. The U-2 was an extremely difficult aircraft to fly. Only the best and most experienced pilots could be selected to be a member of the Black Cat Squadron.

I remember clearly the day Yeh did not return from his mission and I was asked to help package his belongings.

On the way back to Taichung from the welcoming dinner that night, I thought about writing a book on their pathetic experience when I would have time. This thought was not to materialize until I retired and moved to a senior community in the United States. After numerous interviews with Yeh and Chang I realized that time has eroded both of their memories in the past forty years. I have had to consult published writings on the recent history of the People's Republic of China to put together the events they told me in sequence.

Chinese names are always arranged the family name first, followed by the given name (the first name in the United States). The given names are commonly one or two characters. Many translators add a hyphen between the two characters to form the given name, which in the author's opinion is not consistent with the translation of names of places. Therefore, all the hyphens of given names in this book are eliminated. Chinese names are translated phonetically. Traditionally, Wade-Giles Romanization syllabaries are used to translate Chinese names into English. The People's Republic of China invented another system of syllabaries, namely "Pinyin." Therefore, I have translated all the names in mainland China in Pinyin. The rest remain the traditional way. In consideration of protecting personal privacy, I have replaced many names with aliases.

I am very fortunate that my wife, Margaret, reviewed each chapter right after I had finished its first draft. Her comments were a great contribution to this book. I am indebted to Dr. Harold P. Ford for his encouragement and his advice on my writing. Dr. Ford was the Chief of the CIA station in Taiwan from 1965 to 1968, and knew the U-2 operations of the Black Cat Squadron. I am also in debt to Mr. Cargill Hall, the former Chief Historian of the National Reconnaissance Organization, for his valuable editorial comments, which helped me to improve on English usage.

Chapter One: Solitary Confinement

After cleaning the wounds on Major Yeh "Robin" Changti's legs and hips, applying some antibiotic ointment, and covering them with bandages, the nurse told him that he would be discharged from the hospital that day. The message made him suddenly aware that he would soon face an unknown environment, maybe an intolerable one. He could not help to ask the nurse:

"Do you mean I can leave the hospital today? But where will I go?"

Yeh did not know any person in the mainland. He had no money. He did not even know where he was at this moment.

"I don't know. The People's Liberation Army (PLA) will take care of you," the nurse answered sharply.

Yeh, a military pilot of the Republic of China (ROC) stationed in Taiwan, on November 1, 1963, had flown a U-2 photoreconnaissance airplane from Taoyuan Air Base and penetrated the Bamboo Curtain deep into the northwestern provinces of the People's Republic of China (PRC). On the way back, when he had the coastline of southeastern mainland China in sight, he was happy to have almost accomplished this nine-hour mission. It only took another forty minutes to reach the Taiwan Strait and be free of the enemy ground-to-air missile threat. Suddenly, the radar warning receiver on board, System 12, sent a high-pitched signal to his headset, and a light strobe glowed on the two-inch indicator. It alerted Yeh that missile guidance radar had locked on his aircraft in the strobe direction. He had to execute an evasive maneuver immediately. He had successfully evaded the first SA-2 missile, but the second one tore off his right wing and exploded.

He vaguely remembered pulling the D-ring to open the parachute after diving through clouds and seeing the ground, and then made a hard landing in a dry rice paddy. He could not remember anything after that. When he regained his consciousness, he found himself in a hospital. A doctor told him later that he had passed out because of excessive bleeding. Major surgery had removed fifty-nine major pieces of missile fragments from his lower body and, together with a large blood transfusion, saved his life. Many smaller fragments still remained in his body, which might require further surgery in the future.

The nurse helped Yeh to put on a cotton-padded Chungshan suit, first worn by Dr. Sun Chungshan (Sun Yatsen), the leader of Chinese revolution in 1911. Renamed the "Mao suit" after the Chinese Communist Party (CCP) took over the Chinese mainland, Chairman Mao Zedong and his followers wore them all the time. The faded blue color around the collar and cuffs showed someone probably had worn this suit for quite some time before he died in this hospital. Yeh had no choice, as he had almost no clothing of his own.

The U-2 is a fragile, high-altitude reconnaissance airplane. It can cruise above 70,000 feet. Pilots depend on pressure suits for protection, or they would die instantly in the thin air, as blood vaporizes like boiling water at that altitude. The pressure suit worn by U-2 pilot in 1960s were very tight and could hardly be put on without assistance. It had no room for any kind of clothing worn between the suit and the skin except one layer of long johns. The missile explosion had torn all Yeh's clothes, and the only thing left for him to wear was a pair of damaged boots.

He could not remember who put the coarse-cloth underwear on him in the hospital. He sensed the harsh feeling as the underwear rubbing some tender part of his skin; so different from wearing the soft-knit underwear that he had for so many years. Lying on a hospital bed under a comforter, a set of underwear may be enough. To go out of the hospital, he needed heavier clothes in this late autumn weather.

Not long after he had dressed, three men in military uniforms came into his room. One of them wore four pockets on his jacket with red collar insignia, and appeared to be an officer. The other two, in plain uniforms with two pockets on their jackets, must have been enlisted soldiers. The officer approached Yeh and said:

"My name is Kuo Di. I am a Section Chief of the Political Department of the People's Liberation Army Air Force (PLAAF). We are here to take you to our hostel."

"Hostel" sounded like a nice place. What a pleasant surprise! Yeh thought they would move him to some prison. But it did not take long for him to realize that hostel is just a name. It can be a name of any place. It can be the name of prison, dungeon, torture room, or even death row.

Before they were ready to leave, the nurse came in and gave Yeh a package of cotton balls, gauze pads, and a small bottle of Mercurochrome. From now on he had to take care of his unhealed wound by himself. He said to the nurse, "Thank you," as he customarily showed appreciation. She did not respond and did not even change her facial expression slightly.

Yeh felt severe pain around his wounded areas and he was too weak to follow them walking out of the hospital. Kuo must have noticed Yeh's pale complexion and faltering steps. He told the soldiers to help Yeh. Each soldier poked a hand under Yeh's armpits on both sides and lifted him up almost off the ground on the way out.

A black van was parked in front of the gate. The soldiers helped him into the van and closed the back doors. Yeh sat on a side bench between two soldiers. Kuo took the front seat by the side of the driver. There was a metal partition between the driver's seat and the box compartment. A small window with iron bars on this partition was the only opening of the compartment. Yeh could see the driver's head through the small window, and houses moving backward which showed that the van was being driven through narrow streets.

"Where are we going?" Yeh asked the younger soldier on his right, whom he thought might be easier to communicate with.

"Air Force Hostel."

"Where is the Air Force Hostel?"

No answer! The soldier stared at him with a face Yeh had seen so many times since he first woke up in the hospital. He had never seen a smiling happy face on the mainland. They all seemed to have animosities toward others. Why were all the people under the Communist government so different from those Chinese in the rest of the world?

He thought the soldier might not hear what was asked. He repeated the question. The soldier frowned and said:

"Can you stop asking?"

A military hostel is supposed to provide accommodations for traveling military personnel. There should have been no secret about its location. The rude attitude and suffocating surroundings made him very worried about what would happen next. He knew he was in a disastrous situation.

The U-2 was and remains today a most capable spy airplane. It can fly at an altitude that virtually no other airplane of the world can reach. Moreover, it can fly 4,000 miles continuously without refueling. In the 1960s, the pictures taken by its camera from that altitude were exceptionally good, revealing the models of automobiles in a parking lot. On each mission in the 1960s, the airplane could bring back a 2,000-mile-long and 200-mile-wide aerial photographic map containing fine details of the facilities and activities on the ground. Its electronic equipment could collect intelligence about enemy's radar frequencies and locations, and also electronic communications. The U-2 was developed in the United States of America in the 1950s especially for gathering intelligence on Russian nuclear weapon facilities and their delivery vehicles.

Kremlin leaders were embarrassed because no Soviet fighter aircraft could stop American U-2s from flying over Russia. On the other hand, they had no evidence to show the world that the American had intruded into Russian airspace since 1956. Their revenge finally came on May 1, 1960: a U-2 was shot down inside the USSR by newly developed ground-to-air missiles, the SA-2. The U-2 pilot Gary Powers was captured and underwent a public trial. Then, Soviet Premier Khrushchev humiliated President Dwight Eisenhower by demanding an apology at the Paris Summit Meeting. All these events made the U-2 a world-renowned spyplane.

The Republic of China (ROC) in Taiwan and the United States had agreed to use U-2s as vehicles to collect intelligence of military deployment and nuclear weapon development in the Communist China. ROC Air Force pilots were dispatched to the continental United States to learn to fly this aircraft in 1959. A joint squadron was formed with Chinese pilots and American ground operation personnel, with the black cat as its insignia, and then followed by two U-2s being delivered to Taoyuan airbase in Taiwan.

The reconnaissance missions penetrating the Bamboo Curtain started in January 1962. Even though the U-2s cruised at an altitude approximately five miles higher than that the MiGs could reach, and the MiGs could never interrupt the U-2s' photoreconnaissane missions, the People's Liberation Army Air Force (PLAAF) dispatched MiGs to intercept the intruders anyway. The MiGs always followed the U-2 over the mainland, and hopefully some malfunction happened that would force the U-2 to descend to the MiGs' combat zone. The pilot of a U-2 could easily spot an enemy fighter the size of a tiny pinpoint at the tip of a long white contrail over the background of the earth's surface.

In the first six months of overflight, the U-2s had covered the entire Chinese mainland except Sinkiang and Tibet. The top officials in Chungnanhui (中南海 where the Central Committee of the Chinese Communist Party was located) were even more exasperated by these intrusions than were their counterparts in the Kremlin. The People's Liberation Army Air Force had only four USSR-supplied

SA-2 battalions in operation. Four ground-to-air missile battalions could not protect all the important areas in the vast mainland. The split that had occurred between the USSR and the PRC leaders since 1960 had eliminated the possibility of purchasing more SA-2s. PLAAF deployed the battalions to some strategic locations intending to ambush the incoming spyplane. It was difficult to predict where the airplanes would go on the next mission, and the ground-to-air missile equipment was too heavy to move quickly in a short time.

The guessing game had occasionally achieved some results. The first ROC U-2 piloted by Lieutenant Colonel Cheng Huai was shot down by an SA-2 over Nanchang on September 9, 1962. The ChiComs found him fatally wounded. They tried to save him but failed. Yeh was the second pilot downed a year later. He was also the first U-2 pilot captured alive in the Communist China.

For the Republic of China, these missions were vitally important to its security, although the intelligence collected had to be shared with the United States. The ROCAF pilots were patriotically enduring long, hard hours, squeezed into a small cockpit, facing the danger of enemy missiles and the possibility that their own aircraft might malfunction deep inside enemy territory. But to the Communist Chinese, these missions were regarded differently. Mainland radio stations near the Taiwan Strait broadcast messages beginning in July 1962:

"Dear Chinese U-2 Pilots: ... Stop risking your lives to sell the secrets of your motherland to the American capitalists for that bloody money.... Your motherland welcomes you back.... If you fly back with a U-2, we will reward you eight thousand ounces of gold......."

In fact, all Chinese U-2 pilots at that time had been born in mainland China. "American capitalists" were the number-one enemy of the People's Republic of China. To spy for the enemy of the motherland was treason, which definitely deserved capital punishment.

"The only reason for them to keep me alive is the hope of collecting intelligence from me." Yeh spoke silently to himself. He expected these Communists would force him to tell every detail of the joint Chinese-American operation. They might torture him until they were satisfied with the results of interrogation, or until his death.

Earlier, after Chen Huai was shot down over the mainland, the ChiComs made no announcement about what had happened to the pilot, but one of the media reported that Chen had committed suicide with his own pistol when he saw PLA soldiers approaching him. All the U-2 pilots knew the report was ridiculous because they had never carried guns on any mission. However, in the beginning they were told that in the U.S. U-2 missions over Russia, pilots were provided with a lethal pill (called L-pill) molded like a sugar-coated chewing gum, to be used in case of capture and unable to stand the torture. This practice was abandoned after someone found he had mistakenly mixed it with other candies and almost chewed it.

At that moment, Yeh really wished he had one of those pills.

The van stopped at the gate of a compound surrounded by tall brick walls. The soldiers took Yeh through a courtyard into a small room in the right wing. There was a single bed in the middle of the room with its head against a wall. A small, well-worn table and a shabby chair were placed between the bed and a window on the other wall. A toilet and a sink were installed in an alcove on the opposite side of the table. There was a doorframe between the alcove and the room. The door must have been removed and reinstalled as the entrance door to this room, because the wall on the side of the entrance door looked different in its construction material from the other walls of the room. It must have been installed later to partition a regular room with private toilet to become a small detention room separated from a room for guards. The glass window on that door was covered with a curtain on the outside, which provided an opening for guards to watch how the detainee was doing.

Yeh lay down on the bed that was hard as only one layer of cotton blanket on the wooden board. He moved around trying to find a less painful position. He could not remember ever having slept on a bed like this one, even when healthy. Fortunately, there was a comforter, which could provide some cushion.

Through the rusty iron bars on the window he could see a wall and the roofs of other houses. There were some trees on the other side of the wall. The cold wind had stripped all the leaves away and made the branches sway. In this quiet surrounding he could hear some people at a distance talking with a strong Beijing accent. This house must be located somewhere near the capital of the People's Republic of China, Beijing.

On the table there was a red plastic jacket containing four thick volumes inside with the title *The Selected Works of Mao Zedong*. There was also a newspaper. Yeh was curious to read this Communist paper. However, the simplified Chinese printed on the crummy paper made him feel like an illiterate. The only characters he recognized were the date: November 18, 1963. He suddenly realized it was Betty and his first wedding anniversary. Sadness overwhelmed him.

Nine years before, Yeh had graduated from the ROC Air Force Academy and assigned to the 11th Fighter Wing in Hsinchu, Taiwan. The leader of his flight, Major Wen, happened to be a classmate of Yeh's older brother, which made him almost the leader's protégé. He also liked Wen's delightful personality and respected Wen's skill in maneuvering the aircraft. On one special occasion, the 11th Fighter Wing celebrated by inviting all of the officers' dependents and friends to see their operational environment. Wen invited his girlfriend, Hsiaotung. She brought her younger sister along. Wen asked Yeh to accompany the younger sister to see the F-86 Saber fighter, intending to have some private time with his girlfriend. That was the first time that Yeh met Betty.

Betty was a first-year student at a girl's senior high school. She wore the student's uniform: white blouse, black skirt, white socks, and black tennis shoes, with black, straight hair cut to her ear lobes. She looked younger than her age.

Yeh showed her what a fighter pilot wore: the helmet, the oxygen mask, the Mae West, and the anti-G flying suit. Yeh helped seat her in the Saber cockpit. He stood on a ladder by her side and explained patiently all the complicated gauges, control levers, knobs, handles, and switches packed densely around the pilot's seat. She did not understand most of the technical jargon, but she was totally absorbed because this was the first time she had ever been so close to a jet fighter. She was also amazed that a pilot had to monitor so many gauges and manage so many controls at the same time to fly this fighter. Yeh told her that this aircraft could fly faster than the speed of sound while diving. A pilot in that condition will not hear the noise made by the airplane's engine. Betty was sure that she had met a superman. Shyness could not hide her admiration. Yeh was pleased at receiving such an unexpected warm response.

In conservative Chinese society, where co-ed high schools did not exist, adolescent dating in public would cause severe criticism. Betty could not have fallen in love at first sight. Yeh practically had been brought up in an all-male fraternity—a boy's grade school, a boy's high school, and then military academy. This was the first time he had accompanied a girl individually for quite a while. He did not know how to court a person of the opposite sex. Besides, Betty looked too young to be a candidate for being his girlfriend. However, they liked each other and would not miss any opportunity of meeting thereafter.

A youngest member of a big family, Betty had six sisters and one brother. Her brother was spoiled as the only male child. He was supposed to carry the family name for generations to come, an important Chinese tradition. Her brother had all the privileges at home. During the economically disastrous years after World War II, China was so poor that an army major general could not provide sufficient food for his family of nine. Meat and eggs were scarcely seen on the dining table. If any tasty food became available, her parents always let the brother eat first. The girls shared the rest if there were still some leftovers. The brother always thought himself superior to any of his sisters and entitled to absolute authority over his siblings.

As Betty became acquainted with Yeh, she found men were not all rude like her brother. Yeh was gentle and considerate. She also found that he was good in English. She wished Yeh were her big brother.

Yeh's father had been a comptroller under a warlord in Kwangtung Province. The warlord was persuaded to join Generalissimo Chiang Kaishek fight against the Japanese invasion in 1937. Yeh's father moved his family to Hong Kong and he himself followed his boss traveling over the mainland until the Japanese surrender in 1945. Then the whole family moved to Taiwan. Hong Kong was a British colony, and English was the official language there. All the children of well-to-do families were educated in schools where Chinese was only a second language, which provided Yeh a good English background.

From time to time, Yeh did help Betty improve her English. Each time Betty received a better school report, both of them felt rewarded. When Betty graduated from high school, her father had already retired from the army. As he could not support Betty to pursue a college education, she found a job in a local bank. Then she began to date Yeh openly. To see a movie, to taste a good food in a popular restaurant, to tour a scenic spot, to dip in the ocean or to attend a party, there was always a reason for them being together.

One evening, Yeh took Betty to a dancing party, which was routinely held in the Air Force Officers' Club every Saturday night. Probably because Betty had changed her hairstyle and put on light makeup and a becoming dress, he suddenly realized that she was a budding flower. That night they had their first kiss when they said good night.

Early one spring day, they went to Yangminshan Park on the hilly outskirts of Taipei, a very popular place to visit during cherry blossom season. When they arrived there they found the cherry blossoms had been shattered by a storm the night before. Petals were spread all over the ground. The rest remaining on the twigs had turned grayish in color. Only the azaleas under the bright sunshine stole the visitors' hearts. The flowers were fully blooming and covered all their green leaves. The red, pink, and white bushes proudly radiated among the other plants.

The park was very crowded. Yeh and Betty climbed up further toward hilltop to find a quiet place of their own. The rain had cleansed the smog over Taipei city. Above the park, they enjoyed the view of the whole metropolitan city and many beautiful villas scattering on the hillside of Yangminshan. Yeh spotted a single house nearby with brick wall around its small yard. It was only a two-story plain house with no fancy decoration. But its view must be very good as the windows facing Taipei city. Yeh said:

"If we could have a small house like that, I would be very much satisfied."

"If we could have a small house like that, I would plant the whole yard with azaleas," Betty followed.

It seemed natural to say "we" like an engaged couple, instead "you" or "I," although Yeh had never formally proposed to Betty. They both knew a military officer of the Republic of China could be legally married only when he reached twenty-eight years of age. They were pretty sure they would tie their wedding knot at that time, which was less than two years away.

In March 1960, a ROC P2V was shot down over mainland China while executing a clandestine night mission. All thirteen crew on board died. The P2V squadron was stationed in Hsinchu too. Their families were all living in a compound nearby. One of the surviving wives was a close friend of Betty's family. Betty's parents paid a visit to the compound intending to comfort her. They found their condolences were unable to ease her sorrow. They could also hear wailing in nearby homes. Looking around the compound, some had just lost their loved ones, some were widows from previous missions, and some were worrying about their husbands or sons who would undertake future missions. The whole community was despondent.

Betty's parents were deeply depressed by the sad scene and realized how dangerous the profession of military pilots was, especially since the war between the Nationalists and the Communists was still going on. They would certainly not like to see their baby daughter going through the same miserable situation. They decided to persuade Betty not to marry Yeh and started to spend time selecting another prospective son-in-law.

Each time an eligible bachelor was introduced to her by her parents or sisters, Betty always told Yeh in detail about those meetings and asked him for his opinion. Yeh well understood the risk he would take as a patriotic military pilot, and that rationally he should not force her to take the same risk. He never gave her any negative advice until she definitely told him she did not like the new friend. Then they would discuss a strategy to discourage this suitor.

As the political condition of South Vietnam deteriorated in the 1960s and the United States sent more military advisors to help Ngo Dinh Diem's government, Taiwan conveniently became an American intermediate logistic support station. The Office of Military Assistance Advisory Group (MAAG) in Hsinchu expanded and a position of secretary became open. The good salary and prestige of this position attracted many educated women to apply. With Yeh's coaching, Betty won the position. Both of them were extremely happy, since many of the applicants were college graduates.

In early October of 1962 Yeh received a notice that he has been selected to be a U-2 pilot and would be dispatched to the United States to receive training. The U-2 was the most advanced reconnaissance aircraft at that time. It was a great honor for Yeh to be selected to fly this world-renowned aircraft. But he also felt uneasy leaving Betty behind for the six months of training. Without his company, Betty might fall into some other beau's trap. Yeh might lose her forever. He decided not to wait anymore. He went to see Hsiaotung, Betty's elder sister who had introduced Betty to him many years ago, and asked her for help.

Hsiaotung was sympathetic and did try her best to convince her parents. Along with Betty's earnest appeal, her parents finally gave their consent. Yeh and Betty did not waste any time. They had their wedding ceremony ten days later in November 1962. Many guests congratulated them with the Chinese saying "有情人終成眷屬" (Lovers are finally married), as they all knew the bride and groom had been courting for more than eight long years.

The honeymoon can never be long enough. Yeh had to leave for the United States right after the New Year's holidays of 1963. He returned to Taiwan in July and then undertook the combat training in Taoyuan. Betty was still working in Hsinchu. Although it only took forty-five minutes drive from Taoyuan to Hsinchu, they could only see each other on weekends.

The U-2 had been developed quickly in 1954-55, to meet the urgent needs of U.S. national defense during the Cold War. The technical requirements of this aircraft were far beyond state of the art. The designer had to sacrifice pilot's safety and controllability to achieve aircraft's high-altitude performance requirement. Besides dangerous missions penetrating deep into enemy territory, the flying safety record of this aircraft was one of the worst ever in American military history. During its first three years in commission, out of fifty aircraft produced, seventeen U-2s crashed and eleven pilots were killed. Operating in Taiwan, two out of five qualified U-2 pilots lost their lives in less than two years. That was why all the U-2 pilots in Taiwan were promised that they would be promoted to good positions in the ROC Air Force after completed ten photoreconnaissance missions over the mainland China.

Yeh estimated that he would complete the ten missions in two years. He did not want any child of his to be fatherless. So he told Betty that he hoped to begin a family after their second anniversary, but did not tell her why. Betty thought he would just like to enjoy some intimate time for themselves. Indeed, fate intervened: an enemy missile shot him down on his third mission.

The light from the window was getting dimmer as the night fell. Yeh lay on the bed and stared at the cracked ceiling with dangling cobwebs gradually darkening. Reminiscences of happy times with Betty appeared in his vision; one followed another. He remembered a movie that they watched together on their honeymoon, where a loving couple said to each other, "Till death do us part," in their marriage vow. Yeh and Betty both thought that this wording was much stronger than the blessings in a Chinese wedding, such as "愛河永浴" (Immerse in the river of love forever) or "白首偕老" (Enjoy golden years together with white hair). That night they did not say good night, they said, "Till death do us part," instead. Many times at various occasions afterward, they repeated this short phrase as if reaffirming their wedding vow.

He remembered Betty holding his father's arm coming down the aisle. She was so beautiful in that white wedding gown, which her sisters forbade him to see before the ceremony, as they said it would cause him bad luck. Yet bad luck had not been avoided by following the advice of Betty's sisters.

The naked electric bulb hanging down on a wire from the ceiling lit up suddenly. Someone might turn it on with a switch in the other room. The light woke Yeh up from his meditation, but did not interrupt his thoughts about Betty. No words could describe how much he missed her. Over many years he had watched her grow up to be a swan, to be his soul mate, to be his lover, and to be his wife. He spoke to himself, "Till death do us part," again and again, which seemed to strengthen his will power. He had made up his mind, no matter what happened to him, he would use every possible means to survive.

Chapter Two: Interrogation

Through the window of his room Yeh could see a cloudless blue sky. It must be a beautiful autumn day, he thought to himself. The sun had risen above the roofs of neighboring houses and cast a bright column of light down onto the floor and a wall on which was superimposed the shadow of iron bars. He got up from the bed and relaxed on the chair in the sunshine, which brought a warm feeling to him in the chilly climate. He enjoyed the temporal serenity. In this solitarily confined room, he was definitely sure no person with a friendly face would come to see him, yet no immediate threat or humiliation pressed on him, at least that moment.

The squeaky noise of unlatching a lock outside the door alerted him that someone was coming into the room. A soldier opened the door, told him some cadres were waiting to see him in another room, and rushed him to dress.

Yeh followed the soldier out of the room. While passing through the guardroom, he noticed a bunk bed against the left wall. That must be the place where these two soldiers slept overnight, he thought. A window on the other wall faced the courtyard. On a table at the right corner were some sundry items and a set of *The Selected Works of Mao Zedong*. Another set of *The Selected Works of Mao Zedong*! It seemed to Yeh that these red-cover books were in every room in Communist China, just like the King James Version of the Bible found in every hotel or motel room in the United States. But the

Bible was always kept in the top drawer of the nightstand. The red books were displayed like trophies in the most distinct place in the room.

They went through a door next to the table into another room. Three cadres, all wearing baggy blue Mao suits, were sitting behind a rectangular table. Yeh recognized the middle one as Kuo, the cadre who brought him out of the hospital. The soldier led him to a chair about three yards in front of the table and then left the room. The sunlight from the window struck him in the face and made it hard for him to see the other faces in detail. The cadre on the left of Kuo held a pen and some paper, ready to record their conversation. Kuo told the cadre at his right:

"*Hsiao* Zhang, we can start the interrogation now."

"Yes, *Lao* Kuo."

Hsiao (小) means little or junior. *Lao* (老) means old or senior. These addresses are commonly used by peasants and labors or between very close friends. All educated Chinese, since Confucius taught people how to maintain social order two thousand five hundred years ago, traditionally have addressed others by their titles along with family names, such as "Mr. Li" or "Director Wang." They rarely call someone by a first name, unless well acquainted with him or her. Subordinates even call their superiors by title only, without a family name attached, to show their respect. It was obvious that Kuo was the supervisor of Zhang. How dare Cadre Zhang call his boss *Lao* Kuo? Yeh thought, the Communists had made so many changes since they took over the mainland fifteen years ago.

After a few general questions as a matter of formality, such as Yeh's name, age, rank, organization, members of family, and so forth, Cadre Zhang asked:

"What was the objective of your mission?"

"I don't know." Yeh replied.

"How can you say you don't know? You took off from Taoyuan, passing Xian, Lanzhou, flew more than three thousand kilometers to

Jiayuguan. And then returned to Wuhan. What kind of intelligence did you want to collect in order to please the American capitalists?"

Yeh remembered the old Chinese saying "the more you say, the more you lose" (言多必失). He also understood every thing you say will be recorded and will be used against you when the situation is right for the benefit of Communist Party. Back in the spring of 1956, Mao Zedong had announced a policy: "Let a hundred flowers bloom and a hundred thoughts contend" (百花齊放), which meant the guaranteed freedom of speech. He encouraged people to criticize and express any dissatisfaction openly. One year later, all the intellectuals who had criticized Communist Party were arrested and prosecuted. Mao acknowledged that this was the only way to sort out the hidden anti-revolutionaries. Yeh decided to provide as little information as possible; he would have to find an excuse to evade.

Yeh responded, "The U-2 is a top-secret project. We pilots work on 'need to know' basis. Each time we execute a mission, we just fly the aircraft following the courses marked on the map. We don't know the purpose of the mission."

"Don't be so smart!" Zhang snapped. "We all know that U-2 is a photoreconnaissance aircraft. If you don't know the targets, where should you take pictures?"

Yeh, of course, knew all the targets. He knew a nuclear gaseous diffusion plant was located near Lanzhou, which produced the material for atomic bombs. He knew of a test site located near Jiayuguan where the ChiComs were developing their ballistic missiles. He knew the location of numerous military facilities, industries, and many others. But he had to hold the line to avoid further questions.

"We just follow the marks on the map to turn on or off the camera switch."

"Then, who plotted the courses on the map for you?"

"Our navigators."

"Are they Chinese or American?"

"Chinese."
"What are their names?"
"Sun and Yang."
"No Americans were involved?"
"There is an American advisor, I don't know his name."
"Who planned your mission? The CIA?"
"I don't know."

Many questions regarding possible links with the CIA had been asked and followed by many "I don't know"s. As the interrogation dragged on, Cadre Zhang's voice became louder and louder and Yeh's voice became weaker and weaker, until Cadre Zhang finally lost his patience and yelled:

"You stubborn Chiang Kaishek bandits! Do you know how severe is the crime you have committed against the people of China? You have served Chiang Kaishek to prevent our great leader Chairman Mao from liberating the people in Taiwan. You have sold national secrets to American imperialists. You are a traitor to your own country. You think the Americans can protect you. Don't you know that America is a paper tiger? Don't you remember America was defeated by our great Liberation Army in Korea and forced to solicit a truce. It won't be long before the blood of Chiang Kaishek bandits are used to cleanse Taiwan. You had better tell us the truth now. If you are stupid and do not tell us now, sooner or later you will confess. We are patient. We can wait. One of these days, you will be begging for a chance to confess."

Yeh had no answer. The room suddenly became deathly quiet. Time seemed to stand still. Kuo finally broke the silence.

"*Lao* Yeh, I think you are not ready today. You don't know our policy. Our great leader Chairman Mao taught us 'Lenient treatment to those who confess frankly. Severe punishment to those who remain stubborn. Reward to those who provide helpful information.' Go back and think it through."

"Section Chief Kuo, I cannot lie about what I really don't know."

"Don't call me Section Chief. Just call me *Lao* Kuo. We will stop the interrogation now. Go back to think about it thoroughly."

The cadre on Kuo's left opened the door to let the soldiers in. They took Yeh back to his room and latched the door outside.

The next day, a soldier returned Yeh to the interrogation room. He realized Kuo was not there. Yeh thought it is going to be tough today. To his surprise, Cadre Zhang's attitude changed completely. Starting with common greetings, he followed with questions about when Yeh reported to the U-2 squadron, where he learned to fly U-2, and what previous missions he had flown. The interrogation was not hostile as it had been the day before. Then,

"According to our records, each time our surface-to-air missiles' guidance radar turned on, the U-2 turned and started to fly away from the missile site. How did you pilots know that you were approaching a missile site?" Cadre Zhang asked.

"I have said before we pilots work on 'need to know' basis. I don't know what the other pilots did."

"*Lao* Yeh, you have not answered my question! According to our missile battalion, your aircraft started to turn away as soon as our radar switched on. How did you know that it was a missile site?"

Yeh remembered that he was thrown out of the cockpit by the missile explosion and did not have time to press the red button on the instrument panel before leaving the aircraft. That button was supposed to activate a detonator in the equipment bay that would destroy all the electronics. It was highly possible that the PLAAF found System 12 in the aircraft wreckage and had determined its functions. He decided that it was prudent not to deny the existence of System 12.

"There is a small indicator on the instrument panel of U-2," Yeh replied. "We were told when a strobe light appeared on the indicator and a red light flashed on its edge, we should turn the aircraft away from the direction of strobe light."

"How does the indicator know there is a missile site?"

"I don't know. I am a pilot, not an engineer."

"Don't pretend to be stupid. Sooner or later, we PLAAF, under the guidance of our Great Chairman Mao, will find out how that instrument works. Even if we don't know its function, we still can defeat you. Do you know how we shot you down? We deployed four battalions in a row that left you no room to escape!"

The interrogation continued until Cadre Zhang decided it had been enough for that day. The soldier then took Yeh back to his room.

The next day Cadre Zhang asked questions mostly about the operations of the RF-101, which Yeh had piloted before he transferred to the U-2 squadron. Yeh knew that PLAAF had all the information about that operation, because one of the pilots, Major Wu Paotze, was shot down over Fuchow near the southeast coast of China and was captured in August 1961. He later broadcast over the Communist radio, calling RF-101 pilots by name to bring a RF-101 to the mainland and join him. Wu Paotze said that the PLLAF treated him very well, as it surely had after the Communists' brainwash.

The interrogation did not trouble Yeh because he knew there was little to hide about the missions he had executed in RF-101 squadron. Major Wu must have told the PLAAF about them already.

The RF-101 Voodoo is a twin-engine, supersonic reconnaissance aircraft. Yeh was selected and sent to Okinawa for training in this aircraft in 1960. He was the first to fly a photo mission with this aircraft over mainland China in June 1961, and brought back the clear pictures of five newly constructed air bases along the coast. The ample intelligence collected by that flight had been reported to the supreme commander of the ROC armed forces, Generalissimo Chiang Kaishek. The generalissimo then paid a special visit to Taoyuan Air Base to praise Yeh's accomplishment, and took a picture with Yeh in front of the RF-101. It was a great honor for Yeh among his colleagues.

After many questions and answers, Cadre Zhang took two pictures out of his file and asked Yeh to tell him where these pictures were taken and who was in these pictures. It was not difficult for Yeh to recognize the places in these pictures as the officer's club of the RF-101 squadron, and the backyard of the Taoyuan Air Base hostel.

The first picture must have been taken at a dance party, because the pilots and their wives or girlfriends appeared in high spirits. It must have been taken after Wu was captured by the PLAAF, for several of the pilots had not transferred to this squadron when Wu was assigned there. Yeh was pretty sure that Wu had answered the same question already. He has no problem in telling Cadre Zhang the names of the pilots except some of those new ones who came after Wu had left the squadron.

The second picture was most likely taken on a summer weekend. The people in this picture were small. But it was easy for Yeh to tell who they were. A barbecue grill stood on the left of this picture with smoke rising over it. Ed Helsburg, the technical representative (Tech. Rep.) from the Hycon camera company, held a barbecue fork to handle the cooking. On the right of the picture, Russ Eglelon, an American U-2 pilot wearing swimming trunks, stood on the edge of the swimming pool ready to dive into the water. Hugh S___, the manager of the American team; James Travis, the Tech. Rep. from Pratt & Whitney engine company; Colonel Lu, the commander of the Chinese team; Lieutenant Colonel Pao, the Chinese operations officer, and Lieutenant Colonel Yang, a Chinese U-2 pilot, were relaxing on the chairs or recliners in between. All wore T-shirts, and shorts. Some of them held beer cans in their hands.

Yeh told Cadre Zhang "I recognize all of the Chinese in this picture. The Americans are advisors. I usually had little contact with them. I did not ask them for their names or responsibilities. Even had I asked those questions I almost certainly would not get a correct answer."

"To tell you the truth, we know all the names of the people in these pictures," Zhang replied. "I just wanted to show you how capable our PLA intelligence agents are in Taiwan. We know all of the personnel and their duties in your squadron."

Cadre Zhang then read a list of names, ranks, and positions of Chinese personnel in the U-2 squadron, but he did not mention the American participants. Yeh could not tell whether the PLAAF had the intelligence about the Americans, or whether Zhang did not know how to read names in English.

"If you have all the intelligence, why do you bother to interrogate me?" Yeh asked.

"We want to know whether you are telling us the truth."

Yeh had no response, although he was amazed that both the ROC and U.S. counterintelligence could not stop Communist espionage in Taiwan. He had been told not to tell anybody about what he was doing for this joint project, even his wife and parents. He believed every ROC participant had been given the same restriction. At the same time, he thought Cadre Zhang might be just bluffing. The PLAAF might have some intelligence, but definitely not all. They wanted to obtain more intelligence from him, and needed to check whether the intelligence they had was correct by cross-checking with other sources. Yeh still had to answer questions carefully.

The interrogation continued for more than two weeks. Then, without any clue, the soldiers stopped coming to take Yeh to meet Cadre Zhang. However, the next few days, he remained anxious about the interrogations. During the many sessions, he noticed that many questions concerned the same subjects as those asked before, but with different wording. Even for the same wording, Cadre Zhang repeated many times, "*Lao* Yeh, you must have forgotten something. Think again. Think about it thoroughly and tell us the truth. We are patient and wait for your correct answer." It was obvious to Yeh that the questions were intended to ensnare conflicting answers. Conflicting answers would certainly lead to more difficult questions. He had to prepare to answer the similar questions in the future. So he tried to remember every answer he had replied to Zhang's questions and tried to memorize them, over and over. If there were a pen and a notebook available, he would record all the questions and answers in detail for reviewing. He did not want to leave any statement, which the PLAAF could use to accuse him of being a traitor. He would never admit that he knew the intelligence collected would be shared with the "American capitalists."

Probably because Cadre Zhang had run out of questions, or because his threats and yelling could not coerce Yeh into providing any new answers, the interrogation gradually assumed as a routine course. The intervals between sessions became longer and longer. Yeh spent most of his time lying on the bed and watching the small piece of sky in the windrow. The weather changed often. Sometimes in the morning, he saw a layer of frost covering the neighboring roofs under the bright blue sky. Sometimes strong gusts of wind rattled the window in its frame. He could feel the cold air that seeped through the cracks. The comforter kept him warm. The scabs of the wounds were all gone; the scars in their places often itched. He had regained his strength, but he could do nothing to change his situation—except wait.

After about a month, Kuo returned to the interrogation again. After a few questions and answers, Kuo said:

"*Loa* Yeh, you are still not frank with us! We know that your squadron contained more Americans than Chinese. How can you say you don't know what these Americans are doing there? Don't you remember what PLAAF Commander Liu Yalou told you when you were still in the hospital? He said, 'If you want to go back to Taiwan to unite with your family, we will let you go after the investigation is completed. In the meantime, I want you to learn how much the Communist Party has accomplished and how much life in mainland has been improved....' If you don't want to complete the investigation sooner, we have no way to help you."

Yeh vaguely remembered that a group of military personnel who had come to see him in the recovery room after surgery. He was not completely recovered from anesthesia. The man in front wore a tailor-made Mao suit of good quality material, not like those baggy, cotton uniforms worn by the rest of the group. He spoke with authority and said something about returning to Taiwan. No one had introduced him to Yeh. Yeh did not pay much attention to what the man said, as he understood, "If it is too good to be true, it most likely is untrue." However, he was very much surprised to hear another Communist official repeating the same promise. He told himself silently, "When the time is right, I can use this statement to request leaving the mainland." The statement gave him more or less a ray of hope.

"I have told you all I know. I don't think those data which I cannot be sure of are useful to you," Yeh replied.

"You do not trust our Communist Party. You don't appreciate how good we PLAAF have treated you. We saved your life and have helped you recover from your wound. Open your eyes; see how much our Party, under the guidance of our great leader chairman Mao, has contributed to the people of China."

"Incarcerated in a small room, how can I see the great work your Party has accomplished?"

"Don't you read the *Liberation Army Daily* that we provide every day? From now on, you read them and write down your comments. *Hsiao* Zhang, you criticize his comments and teach him to appreciate our Communist Party."

Sometimes Yeh had felt so bored just staring at the sky outside the window, he did pick up the *Liberation Army Daily* and tried to understand the Chinese in simplified characters. It was really not a newspaper in the normal sense. It was a means of indoctrination. The only news told how much the people, under the guidance of Chairman Mao, sacrificed to build a road, a dam, or to produce a huge crop. The editorials always criticized someone's counterrevolutionary thought or behavior, or encouraged people to root out hidden reactionaries. He soon lost interest in reading it.

"Do you have anything else to say?" Kuo asked at the end of the interrogation.

"I know the Communist Party has treated me well. But the weather is getting colder and my clothes are not enough for the winter."

"*Hsiao* Zhang, you take care of this."

A week later, Cadre Zhang brought him some heavy clothes and daily necessities. He said, "Chairman Mao taught us to treat the prisoners of war well. You are to be provided as if you were our junior cadre. Besides, you also will receive six Renminbis (RMB, Chinese currency; six RMB equal a little more than a U.S. dollar) each month. I will keep the money for you. You can let me know when you are short of something. I will tell the soldier to buy it for you."

Yeh then started to read the newspaper as pastime and to write comments occasionally. Cadre Zhang sometime criticized his comments, always concluding that Yeh thought as a bourgeois, a sure sign of decadence in Communist China.

One day in late December 1963, the newspaper reported that Yuie Zhenghua, commander of the Second Missile Battalion, had been awarded the medal "PLAAF Combat Hero (空軍戰鬥英雄)," for shooting down Yeh's U-2. It also included an interview with this newly named hero, about how he had led the battalion to search for methods to shorten the time between turning on the radar and shooting the missiles, in order to reduce the possibility of the U-2 escaping. He had made the tough decision to hold the radar off until the last minute, before they lost entirely the opportunity of shooting. The report did mention where the wreckage of the aircraft had been found, but not how the pilot was.

Yeh hoped the report would reveal that the pilot had been captured alive. In that case, the Communist sympathetic newspaper in Hong Kong would most likely quote the report, and Betty might then be informed Yeh was still alive! But nothing about him appeared in the paper. He read that report several times but could not find a slightest clue. He became quite depressed in the following days.

As the days went by, the tension between himself and the guards was gradually relaxed. Yeh learned the younger soldier was named Wang. He was eighteen years old. He was the only person Yeh could speak a few words with daily when he delivered meals to Yeh. The meals generally included corn grits or millet porridge and pickles for breakfast, steamed buns or rice with greens or tofu for the main meal of the day at noon, and thick rice porridge or noodle soup in the evening. Because of lack of fat and protein, although Yeh ate until quite full, he always felt hungry before the next meal. On the Chinese New Year's Day, the main meal was boiled dumplings stuffed with meat and vegetables. Yeh enjoyed it very much and later spoke to Soldier Wang:

"The dumplings tasted so good. Do you enjoy them?"

"I don't know. We soldiers dine in the mess hall. Your food is provided by the small kitchen for cadres. Don't you know your food is always better than ours? Our food is mainly made from corn or sorghum. We regard rice or a bun as a special treat," Wang replied.

"Even having these meals, I always feel hungry before the next meal. Don't you feel hungry sometimes?"

"Hungry? I don't think you know real hunger."

Wang then told Yeh that he lived in the hilly country of a western province before he joined the army. Food was always scarce before the harvest season. People had to eat grass roots or tree bark to survive. That food never satisfied, even if you fully filled your stomach. The situation deteriorated further when a famine spread all over China in 1961. Wang then joined the PLA, for the Communists always treated soldiers better than civilians.

Wang finally said, "We are fortunate to have Chairman Mao providing us food, unlike the people living in Taiwan, who have only banana peels to eat."

Wang's last statement almost made Yeh laugh. He asked, "If everybody eats banana peels, then where does the banana flesh go?"

Wang suddenly realized the ill logic and said, "Well, that's what our leading cadre told us."

The next morning, Cadre Zhang appeared and rebuked Yeh for planting "a poisonous weed" in the revolutionary garden. Wang was then replaced by another soldier, for failing to "draw a distinct line between revolutionaries and counterrevolutionaries." Yeh realized his every move in this small room had been watched and reported to the higher authorities.

From that incident on, Yeh noticed the guards were changed frequently. He could almost be sure to see new faces at the beginning of a new month.

It was at this time that Communist China pressed the "Learn from Lei Feng" movement. Lei Feng, a common soldier, had a miserable childhood. Yet he sacrificed himself to help the needy and had died at the age of twenty-two. His diary was full of devotion to Chairman Mao and with pledges to follow Mao's leadership without limit and to smash the class enemy mercilessly. The newspaper frequently reported various activities of this movement: school children helped the coolies push heavily loaded carts along rocky roads; groups of people fasted to save their food rations for those in real hunger; someone in his group "recalling grievances" meeting revealed what torture he had endured by the landlord in the "man-eating days of the Kuomintang" (KMT, 國民党, the People's Party, which was led by Dr. Sun Yatsen, later by Chiang Kaishek), and then attendees of that meeting were so moved that they pledged to hate and crush all class enemies; members of another group solemnly declared that they would follow Chairman Mao's order to fight against class enemies until their last breath.....

Who were these class enemies? No clear definition was offered. All of the landlords and their families had been either executed or stripped of all possessions. Yeh especially could not agree with all these accusations against KMT. The landlord and peasant relationship had existed in China for more than two thousand years. It was not created by the KMT, which also had advocated that peasants, not a few landlords, should own the land. The KMT had accomplished land reform in Taiwan without any bloodshed.

Early in the twentieth century, the KMT had led the revolution that overthrew the Qing Dynasty, united the whole country in spite of warlords' obstruction of a central government, won the war against the Japanese invasion, and lifted up the country from sub-colonial status to be one of the five founders of the United Nations. The only crime the KMT committed was losing the war against Communists. The Communists discredited all the KMT merits.

Yeh could not write any comments on the news reports of the "learn from Lei Feng" movement. Cadre Zhang persistently tried to educate Yeh that the movement was important to the masses. From some other news reports about the KMT possibly assaulting the mainland to stage a comeback with the assistance of the United States, Yeh understood that one of the reasons to conduct this movement was to teach the populace to hate the KMT. Several years later, Yeh realized the main purpose of this movement was to recruit the young generation to join the Mao's cult to support him in the forthcoming political struggle. The whole story of Lei Feng was a hoax. The published diary, along with some poems, was impossible—written by an uneducated peasant. The illustrated photos of Lei Feng's good deeds could not have been taken without some official prearrangement, as no camera was available in poor rural society in China that time.

Summer heat made the small room stuffy. Yeh sat near the window to get the cool evening breeze. The soldier brought in the evening meal and the *Liberation Army Daily*. A title of a topic, "Another Chiang Kaishek bandits' spyplane has been shot down by our gallant PLAAF," caught his eyes. It did not mention what kind of aircraft or what brought it down, except that wreckage was found near the coast of Fujian Province. The report, dated July 8, 1964, emphasized "any attempt to invade PRC by Chiang Kaishek bandits is bound to fail."

A few days later, Kuo came to show Yeh a gold ring with the name "Yeh Chiuying" (葉秋英) engraved on it. Yeh immediately recognized it to be Lee Nanping's wedding ring. Lee wore this ring all the time. Yeh Chiuying was Lee's wife's name.

Lee was a close colleague of Yeh. They worked in the same RF-101 reconnaissance squadron, later went to the United States to undertake U-2 training, and then transferred to the U-2 squadron together. Lee must be the pilot of the aircraft brought down recently. The troubled aircraft must be another U-2.

Yeh remembered that in early September 1962, Lee and Yeh had been dispatched to Kadena USAF Base in Okinawa to fly in an RF-101 simulator for all-weather flight training. Before leaving Taiwan, Chen Huai, another Nationalist U-2 pilot, asked them to bring back something that an American friend of Chen bought for him. About a week after they had arrived in Okinawa, the sad news of Chen's U-2 lost deep inside the mainland came. Both of them felt a great loss, as Chen was always nice to friends. No one thought of the fact that all three of them were destined to have the same fate in store—one after another was shot down by missiles while flying U-2 missions over the mainland in the following two years.

Lee was Yeh's senior by three years. He had married and his family, wife, and two lovely children lived in the government provided house near Taoyuan Air Base. Yeh was very close to Lee's family before he himself married. He visited their home frequently. Lee's wife, Yeh Chiuying, was a plain housewife with a warm heart. The news of her husband's catastrophe must have hit Yeh Chiuying severely, Yeh thought, as she used to see her husband every day; even her husband could not stay home overnight for official duty. Not like Betty, who had been living with her parents for all her life. The comfort given by Betty's parents and sisters, and the sympathy bestowed by office colleagues might help her going through the difficult time. It had been more than eight months since he had lost his freedom. Yeh hoped Betty had completely recovered from sorrow.

Kuo asked, "*Lao* Yeh, have you ever seen this ring?"
"Yes, where did you find this ring?"

"That is not important. Do you know who has this ring?"
"The ring belongs to my colleague Lee Nanping."
"Write down his name on this paper."
Yeh did what Kuo said and then,
"Is he the pilot of the aircraft downed few days ago? How is he now?"
"I cannot tell you for the time being. Are you sure this is Lee Nanping's ring?"

Even Kuo did not tell what happened to the pilot; Yeh suspected that Lee might be dead already. Lee's body might have been disfigured beyond recognition. Otherwise Kuo would not come to show him this ring and asked him who the owner was.

Chapter Three: Social Unrest

The cold northwestern wind rattled the window against its frame again. It had been almost a year since Yeh had been incarcerated in this small room. The autumn harvest must have been quite good, as Yeh noticed the quality of the daily meals had improved recently. China had gradually overcome the three-year famine. The *Liberation Army* newspaper devoted most coverage to the fifteenth national anniversary of the People's Republic of China, from preparation to celebration, praising the merits of the Communist Party.

The meetings with Cadre Zhang became more like indoctrination sessions, or even political discussions. Cadre Zhang rarely asked Yeh any questions on U-2 operation, as the interrogator probably thought he could obtain no new answers. During one meeting with Kuo, Yeh said:

"*Lao* Kuo, I think the investigation has been completed. When can I go back to Taiwan? I would like to reunite with my wife and parents."

"Remember Commander Liu told you to learn more about the progress in China. We haven't heard any favorable comments on this subject from you yet."

"Confined in this small room, how can I appreciate your accomplishments?"

"The *Liberation Army Daily* did not tell you all the good deeds?"

"The news is all so good. It is hard to believe they are not exaggerating."

"*Lao* Yeh, I did not know you would remain so stubborn."

The talk went nowhere. However, about two weeks later, Zhang told Yeh to pack his belongings and prepare for transfer.

"Where am I going?" Yeh asked.

"To a hostel in Beijing."

"Why should I move to there?"

"I don't know. It is an order."

This order caused Yeh some degree of suspicion, although he was not as frightened as when he had been told to leave the hospital. A year in confinement made him wiser. There was no use to worry about the future, which he had no way to predict.

A black van took Yeh, along with Cadre Zhang and a soldier, to a single house inside a gated compound. The house had its own exterior walls and gate. In the living room, Zhang said to another cadre who came to greet them:

"*Lao* Zhao, from now on Yeh Changti is yours."

Yeh was then led through an anteroom to a small room. He noticed two soldiers were in the anteroom. He understood this was the place Cadre Zhang called "the hostel in Beijing," a confined room for him to stay for the days to come.

The room was a little bit larger than the previous one and seemed in better condition. Besides the red-jacketed *The Selected Works of Mao Zedong* on the table, there was a small red book, *Quotations of Chairman Mao*, as small as the size of a hand's palm. The bright color of the plastic cover was eye catching. In the room Yeh could hear a broadcast from a distant loudspeaker. Occasionally the speaker would report the news, an instruction, or indoctrination from the county government, followed by some revolutionary songs.

Cadre Zhao and the guards did not look as hostile as the previous team. However, Cadre Zhao seemed to be a devoted follower of

Mao. He always carried the little red book in his pocket. Each time he came to criticize Yeh's comments on some news articles, he always asked Yeh to bow down in front of a chairman Mao's picture hanging on the wall of the living room and read a quotation from the little red book together, before starting the discussion. Yeh thought this must be the ritual of the Communist Party, just as a Catholic often kneels down in front of the altar before his prayer or meditation in a cathedral or a pastor recites a verse from the Bible before preaching. He could not refuse following suit.

In addition to the newspaper, the loudspeaker provided more information about the daily life in the neighborhood around the hostel. People seemed content with the improvements in living condition. No one criticized the ridiculous "Great Leap Forward" movement led by Chairman Mao, which had devastated the economy of the whole country. Many voices were blaming the drought, a natural calamity, which brought residents of the country to the edge of starvation. Some argued that the tragedy was the result of not following Chairman Mao's teaching to root out capitalism totally. Others condemned the mismanagement and corruption of functionaries in the rural areas.

Wang Kwangmei, wife of the president of PRC, Liu Shaogi, visited the countryside and wrote an outstanding report, "The Experiences of Tao Yuan," elaborating the corruption of the rural functionaries. A nationwide campaign named "four cleanups" then began, and thousands of urban cadres and intellectuals were sent to poor rural areas to clean up financial accounting, food distribution, property divisions, and the recording of work points.

Meanwhile, the editorials of the *Liberation Army Daily* continued advocating Mao's socialism against capitalism. Lin Biao, the minister of defense, frequently praised Chairman Mao as the greatest leader, the greatest commander, the greatest teacher, and the greatest helmsman. He ordered all in the PLA to obey Mao's instruction. In return for Lin's flattery, Mao declared, "The merit of the People's Liberation Army is its correct political ideology. The whole nation should learn from Marshal Lin Biao and the PLA."

In late December 1964 the newspaper reported a KMT's RF-101 was crippled by a MiG-19 over Wenzhou in Zhejiang Province. The pilot, named Hsieh Hsiangho, was rescued by a PRC fisherman after bailing out over the ocean. A picture in the report showed the pilot wearing a dark green flying suit standing in front of two PRC soldiers with rifles in their hands. Yeh knew Hsieh very well, for Hsieh was a junior colleague in the RF-101 squadron.

A few days after the New Year's Day in 1965, the newspaper reported that another KMT U-2 had been shot down. This would be the fourth U-2 lost over the mainland. The report described how the missile battalion cadres, combining intelligence and tactics, shot down this U-2 in the middle of night. The wreckage of this aircraft was found in the Nei Mongol (Inner Mongolia) area. Nothing was mentioned about what happened to the pilot, just like the previous U-2 cases. Yeh could not guess who the pilot might be, since three senior pilots had already completed their assignments and were ready to be transferred to other outfits when he flew his last mission. No other pilot was available at that time, except Lee Nan-ping, who had been killed six months ago.

About two months later, another RF-101 was shot down by a Communist MiG-19 near Shantou in Guangdong Province. The pilot, Chang Yupao, was reported killed.

The next day, Cadre Zhao arrived in high spirits to talk about the successive victories of the PLAAF air defenses against intruded KMT aircraft, followed by a lengthy propaganda speech. Yeh had no words in reply.

Yeh noticed that the PLAAF treated U-2 pilots and RF-101 pilots differently. They never released information about what happened to the pilots of the downed U-2s, but always reported details about those downed in RF-101s. It was probably because the operation of the U-2 and the RF-101 were different: the former was a joint project of ROC and the USA, the latter solely controlled by ROC.

If that was the case, U-2 pilots might be regarded by the PLAAF as having some political value in negotiations with the U.S. someday. Yeh knew that the PRC had kept a diplomatic channel with U.S. open in Poland, since the Korean cease-fire agreement in 1953. He could expect to be treated better than the average RF-101 prisoner pilots: Wu, Hsieh, and Chang Yupao. However, Yeh had a mixed feeling, since Betty would have to wait an indefinite amount of time to learn that he was still alive.

He remembered that after twenty-one months of incarceration, Gary Powers, pilot of the American U-2 shot down over the Soviet was released back to the United States in exchange for a Russian spy, Colonel Rudolf Abel, who had been arrested in the U.S. by the American central intelligence. It was very hard for Yeh to guess whether the PRC would use him as a commodity in exchange for some kind of concession from Taiwan or the U.S. Nevertheless, unless the PRC told the other side that Yeh was alive; this exchange would never happen.

Each time Cadre Zhao sought to make a point, he always recited a quotation from the little red book, no matter whether the quotation was applicable to the argument or not. Yeh thought it must be the best way to survive in this Communist country. He started to read the little red book and *The Selected Works of Mao Zedong*, despite the fact that many statements in them were totally unacceptable to him. He soon found that many of Mao's statements, probably written at various times and focusing on different subjects, were not consistent with each other. Their meaning was often vague and could be interpreted to suit one's own preference. There appeared to be leeway in using these quotations for Yeh's own benefit.

A plum tree was blooming in the backyard in the spring of 1965. The warmer weather made Yeh feel more at ease. Kuo came to see him.

"Haven't seen you for quite some time, *Lao* Kuo. How have you been?"

"Busy, busy! Chairman Mao said, 'The whole nation should learn from the People's Liberation Army.' We in the Political Department are responsible for dispatching teams to schools, industries, and communes to teach them the thought of the Chairman. We are all busy on this mission. I don't know when it will be completed. By the way, I am glad to hear that you have been studying Chairman Mao's publications and the little red book," Kuo replied.

They then talked about what Yeh had learned from these readings. Although Kuo could not agree with Yeh's interpretations, he seemed happy about Yeh's apparent attitude change. At the end of their conversation, Kuo said to Cadre Zhao:

"I think you can take Yeh to see some movies or show him the progress in town when you have time."

Good news! At least Yeh would have a chance to get out of this detention house.

On one evening Cadre Zhao led Yeh and a soldier walk to a nearby theater. The dilapidated interior did not surprise Yeh. The noise and crowd inside was a new experience for him. The soldier found three seats in the back row. Yeh sat between Zhao and the soldier. It was probably Yeh's southern accent that attracted attention; a man in the front row looked back at them. The soldier yelled at him immediately, "What are you looking at? Mind your own business!" The man reluctantly turned his head back without a word.

The movie was lousy compared with what Yeh used to see in Taiwan, much less the Hollywood movies. The theme was revenge against capitalist exploitation: A beautiful farm girl was abused by her landlord and landlord's son until a valiant Communist came to her village. The Communist with the girl's help stirred up hatred among the peasants. The whole family of landlord was then prosecuted and all their belongings were distributed. The girl and the Communist were finally married and joined the Revolutionary Army. The conversation in the movie sounded like shouted slogans. Yeh felt oppressed by the propaganda, which was devoid of entertainment. But the audience seemed to enjoy it very much. Yeh surmised that there was no other entertainment.

After seeing several movies in the same format, Yeh lost all the interest in attending movies, especially because the air in the theater was polluted with cigarette smoke and became stuffier as the weather became warmer. Only the stroll to and from the theater was a pleasant alternative to the monotonous life cooped up in a small room.

PLAAF collected all of the debris from the four crashed U-2s, reassembled it in the close shape of four airplanes, and displayed them in front of the military museum. Cadre Zhao led Yeh along with a soldier to see this exhibition. The waiting line was long. Many policemen walked back and forth to direct the crowds to move forward. It required patience to stay in line under the hot summer sunshine. They finally arrived at the front of the display. The four U-2s were parked one after another. The spectators were not allowed to go near the aircraft. However, the aircraft looked bigger in this congested area. Some spectators must have been disappointed, since there was little to see except the disfigured wreckage.

"What a waste of our time! Are these really the U-2 high-altitude spy airplanes? If they did shoot down these aircraft, where are those pilots?" One spectator said.

Cadre Zhao smirked at Yeh and said:

"That stupid idiot doesn't know the pilot is here."

Then they went into the museum to see Chen Huai's pressure flying suit and helmet, along with other remains of U-2s.

The autumn air in Beijing was crisp. The Mongolian wind blew away the smog and turned the color of the treetops. Cadre Zhao and a soldier took Yeh to tour the National Museum of History, which is located east of Tiananmen Square. Tiananmen (天安門) is the southern gate of the Forbidden City, which was the palace of emperors. The square is the open area south of Tiananmen. A memorial to revolutionary martyrs stands on the opposite end of Tiananmen. The Great Hall of People covers all the west side of the square. The Museum of History covers the east of the square. They got off the bus nearby and walked to the square. Cadre Zhao told him the square could hold half a million people. Inside The Great Hall of People there were an auditorium with ten thousand seats and twenty-nine huge conference rooms named for the twenty-nine provinces of China. The awesome view of the vast emptiness and the mammoth buildings around the square impressed Yeh greatly. He had never been in any place like this before. He could almost agree that the Chinese Communist Party (CCP) had accomplished something special for this country.

They spent quite some time inside the museum. Some of the exhibitions irritated Yeh very much. How could the CCP have rewritten modern Chinese history? He had a clear memory of the eight years when millions of Chinese civilians were massacred during the Japanese invasion. The Chinese government led by Generalissimo Chiang Kaishek, in spite of inferior military equipment and manpower, persistently fought against the enemy. He had listened to his father and Betty's father telling the war stories many times of the valiant fighting against the Japanese, and the stories of how the CCP was uncooperative during that rough time. Yeh also remembered that the Japanese armed forces deployed in China had surrendered to the KMT government (國民政府), not the CCP, when the war ended in 1945. But the exhibition showed the CCP had won the war against Japan. Anything related to KMT was corruption and exploitation of labors and peasants.

People might still have fresh memories of the difficult life during the famine years. They felt fortunate to have enough to eat now. The Chinese New Year of 1966 was celebrated warmly. However, political unrest was simmering, as many commentaries appeared in the newspapers, arguing whether a popular Beijing Opera *Hai Rui Dismissed from Office* (海瑞罷官) was a pure performance of art excellence or a political undercurrent. Hai Rui had been an impeccably honest official, extremely loyal to his country in the Ming Dynasty, who was purged for his openness in criticizing the emperor's unsound policies. In 1959 Marshal Pong Dehuai had criticized Chairman Mao's "Great Leap Forward" movement that formed peasant commune and smelted steel in the backyard furnaces.

He was then demoted from the position of defense minister and later imprisoned. The opera seemed to underscore the retaliation against Pong, as he became the Hai Rui of modern age. Mao's wife, Jiang Qing, led a group of left-wing ideologists who filthily attacked the author of this opera, the Beijing vice-mayor. The fundamental conflict appeared to be between the pragmatic executive branch, led by President Liu Shaoqi, and the hardliners of the Communist Party, led by Mao himself. Many new political terms gradually appeared in publications and broadcasting, such as capitalist-roader, revisionist, ox-devil and snake-demon, Cultural Revolution, etc.

In late spring, a document was approved by the Central Committee of the CCP to be the guideline of the "Great Proletarian Cultural Revolution." This movement targeted all bourgeois elements within the Party, the government, and the army. Chairman Mao's Red Guards started to be organized in schools. All classes were suspended. Teachers and school administrators were the first group being criticized and humiliated.

In July 1966 Chairman Mao swam openly in the Yangtze River near Wuhan. The news overwhelmingly surprised many people, as he was seventy-three years old and the current in that area was always swift. Besides, he had not been seen in the public for several years since the failure of "Great Leap Forward." Yeh remembered that people worshiped him like a distant god and quoted his teachings frequently, but Yeh had never read any report about what Chairman Mao had been doing physically or conducting any political activities since Yeh landed on the mainland. Less than a month after the picture of Chairman Mao bobbing in the water appeared in the *Liberation Army Daily*, Mao stood on the top of Tiananmen many times to receive millions of Red Guards from all over the country to worship him in the square. All these showed that Mao was back in control again.

One day Kuo came to see Yeh in late September. Kuo had not come to review Yeh's situation for quite some time because he had been promoted to a higher position with more responsibilities.

Yeh thought he should make use of this opportunity to ask about repatriation.

"*Lao* Kuo, I have been confined in a small room for almost three years. I think I have seen all the wonderful achievements of your Party. When can I be released to go back to Taiwan? You know I have wife and parents there. The American U-2 pilot Gary Powers, captured by Russians, was released back to America in less than two years."

"*Lao* Yeh, you have to be patient. All the high cadres are very busy. Don't you know the Great Proletarian Cultural Revolution is at full swing now?"

"There were so many movements in China. I think the Cultural Revolution is just another movement. If my case has to be approved by high authorities, could you please appeal for me?"

"This movement is completely different. You will see it. As a matter of fact, there will be another rally in Tiananmen Square next week. *Lao* Zhao, try to get a permit for *Lao* Yeh to see the rally."

This permit was not easy to obtain, but three weeks later Yeh was called to get up before dawn. Cadre Zhao and a soldier rushed Yeh into a jeep. After a ride, they stopped at the side door of a building. The guards at this building carefully checked the document Zhao carried and searched everybody. Then they walked up to the second floor. Through a window, Yeh could see all of Tiananmen Square. It was just about daybreak. Yeh could see the whole square covered with an ocean of black heads. If what Zhao said was right, there must be half a million students sitting cross-legged on the hard ground of the square. Many of them looked only thirteen or fourteen years old. Each one wore a red armband with "Red Guard" on it in golden calligraphy. Military personnel led them in singing revolutionary songs, reading Mao's quotations, and shouting Red Guard slogans to keep their spirits up, as many of them were very tired, probably because of exhaustion due to long way traveling or not much sleep the night before. Around Tiananmen Square, Big Character Handwriting Posters (大字報) had been pasted on many bare walls. Ugly vegetables had replaced all the beautiful rose blossoms in front of the Great Hall of People, which Yeh had a good impression of when he visited here last year.

After waiting for hours, the black heads near Tiananmen started to rise. Those who were behind followed them. Everybody raised his right arm and waved Mao's little red book. Everybody shouted, "Long live Chairman Mao!." Yeh could recognize Mao standing at the top of Tiananmen. Lin Biao stood a step behind him and waved the little red book too. Soon shouting became screaming, and then crying. Many in the crowd fainted. The scene scared Yeh. How could half a million people suddenly go into a trance altogether? The communists did have a way of manipulating people's minds.

After Mao and his entourage disappeared from the top of Tiananmen, Yeh followed Zhao to go back by bus. Yeh realized that China had really changed because of the Cultural Revolution movement as Kuo had said. Everybody had to show the little red book along with the ticket before getting on bus. Many people, not only students, wore red armbands. Big Character Handwriting Posters pasted conspicuously all over the spare walls announced: "Smash the so-and-so capitalist-roader," "Annihilate the so-and-so revisionist," "Destroy the so-and-so reactionary bourgeois authority."

At an intersection, Yeh's bus stopped for a parade, which was proceeding on the crossroad. A drum corps led the parade, followed by a group of Red Guards shouting Mao's quotations: "Rebellion is justified," "Destroy an old world so a new one can be born," "Crush the class enemies mercilessly otherwise they will reappear." The main scene in the parade was a group of victims at its end. They wore dunce's caps and their hands were tied behind their backs. Everyone had a large plaque tied to his neck and hanging in front of his chest with humiliating words on it. Some Red Guards pushed or dragged them along the way. They must be some intellectuals, for "Stinking *Lao Geo*" (臭老九) was written on their dunce's caps. *Lao Geo* was the name given by Mao to the intellectuals whose social status was categorized as the ninth-class citizen. Stinking *Lao Geo* referred to those stubborn intellectuals who failed to follow Mao's teaching and were also regarded as one of the class enemies.

On the way from the bus stop to the hostel, they walked through the street where Yeh used to go for the movies. He suddenly remembered that Cadre Zhao had not taken him to see a movie for more than four months. He asked:

"*Lao* Zhao, when you will have time to take me to see a movie again?"

"There is no movie showing here. The theater is now used as an auditorium for struggle meetings."

"There must be too many struggle meetings going on to spare time for movies."

"There will be even more in the future." Zhao predicted.

The so-called struggle meeting was a Communists' arrangement to rally the masses. In the early stage of the revolution, they assembled peasants to watch how the landlords and rich peasants were prosecuted. The meeting then became a way to torture so-called class enemies. They forced the victim wearing the humiliating costume to kneel on the stage with head down and hands tied behind his back. Some people in the audience, incited by the Communists, would come out to accuse him with insulting language for his alleged crimes, which might never have been committed. They forced him to admit, confess, and repent. The show rarely ended without beatings or other kinds of torture.

Cadre Zhao's prediction was right. Eight Red Guards rallies took place in front of Tiananmen in the latter part of 1966, and the number in attendance grew every time. The biggest rally was reported to have had two and a half million students participating. They had to occupy, in addition to the square, the ten-lane Changan Avenue, which runs east and west through Beijing just in front of Tiananmen. Chairman Mao reviewed them on a jeep. Lin Biao made a speech at one of these Tiananmen Square rallies calling on the Red Guards to charge out of their schools to smash all "old ideas, old culture, old customs, and old habits." With Mao's endorsement and the PLA's support, Red Guards openly raided suspected class enemies' houses throughout the country. They destroyed art works and antiques, burned books, and humiliated the owners in the struggle meetings. The police Chief announced, "If some Red Guards hate the class enemies so much as to kill them, we police don't have to stop it." Soon the laborers and peasants organized their own Red Guards and joined the chaos. It was impossible to prevent some hoodlums from using this opportunity to loot and take revenge on their adversaries.

The loudspeaker near Yeh's house must have been taken over by the Red Guards. Besides reciting Mao's quotations three times a day, it now blasted continuously with Red Guards' slogans and accusations against so-and-so as a class enemy. Sometimes Yeh could hear the noise of beating drums and gongs passing by the street. He knew that must be another Red Guard parade and then someone would be tortured in the theater.

From those broadcasts Yeh finally understood that class enemies included anyone identified as landlords, rich peasants, counterrevolutionaries, bad elements, rightists, traitors, foreign agents, capitalist-roaders, or intellectuals. If Red Guards came to investigate his case, he would certainly be accused as a rightist, a traitor, a foreign agent, a capitalist, and an intellectual. He could not imagine what kind of torture he would have to endure. It all depended on whether the PLAAF would release his personal file to the Red Guards or not. This was a continuous threat to him day by day. The detention room might be the safest place for him to stay, at least during the Cultural Revolution.

The target of the Red Guard's prosecution gradually changed towards Party members. In early 1967, both the broadcast media and the newspapers started to accuse some of the top officials in the executive branch of the government. They accused President Liu Shaoqi of being the leader of "Russian Revisionists" and called him "China's Khrushchev." A few months later, he was removed from the presidency and "struggled against" by Red Guards in front of the State Council Auditorium. The police and the military personnel standing around did not provide any help to stop the persecution.

In September 1967, another U-2 was shot down over the south of Shanghai. Probably because the news media was concentrated on the

Cultural Revolution, the report of the victory of PLAAF's surface-to-air missile over the high-altitude spyplane was only published in a corner of the *Liberation Army Daily*. It was not headline news anymore. It did not mention what happened to the pilot, as before. The news told Yeh that the U-2 operation was still going on. He should not expect to be released soon.

The Red Guards were not rigorously organized and different factions had different objectives and different interests. It was impossible for these various factions to campaign in the same society without conflict. They had no way to compromise. Every faction claimed it was authentic Chairman Mao Red Guard. All the factions used Mao's quotations to justify their actions, but Mao's quotations were not consistent and could be interpreted as completely different meanings. Quarrels and fistfights, even fights with arms, happened more frequently as time went on. Many Red Guards were killed in schools, in factories, and in streets. The whole country fell into chaos. The life of the people deteriorated continuously. As his rival, Liu Shaoqi, was gone, and chaos was spreading, Mao did not need Red Guards anymore. Starting from summer of 1968, the leaders of various Red Guards factions were sent to the countryside for further education, followed by millions of Red Guards. Mao said, "Revolutionaries had to learn from the poor and lower-middle-class peasants." The PLA was authorized to clean up the mess and to restore order in the country. It consequently sent teams to take control of government offices and work units at all levels.

In the meantime, Cadre Yang replaced Cadre Zhao. Yang did not come to watch Yeh often as Zhao did, and never mentioned taking Yeh to see some CCP's achievements, but asked Yeh to strictly recite Mao's quotations three times a day. He wore a big Mao button on his upper left pocket, greeted other person with "Long live Chairman Mao!," instead of "Morning!" (早) or "How are you?" (你好). The awkward attitude made Yeh remember the scene in the movie of the Allies' war against Germany. The Nazi officers always greeted others by raising their right arms and howling, "Heil Hitler!" In this situation, Yeh had little to do but lie on the bed, staring at the ceiling and thinking of Betty and his parents. Many times he gazed at the cracks in the ceiling, like a fortuneteller reading someone's fate from the lines in his palm, to search for a line that merged, split, or intersected with other lines to tell his past and hopefully to reveal some signs of his future. Besides that, Yeh could only read the newspapers and listen to the broadcasts from the loudspeaker down the street. He tried to read between the lines what was really going on outside of his small room.

In the spring of 1969, Lin Biao acquired a new title, "Chairman Mao's closest comrade," and was officially designated Mao's successor. Cadre Yang was so exhilarated to tell Yeh the news. The status of the whole PLA seemed to be upgraded too. Military uniforms came into fashion to replace the red armbands.

About the same time, there were armed skirmishes between the Soviet Union and PLA along the Heilongjiang border. Lin Biao issued his "Order Number One" to mobilize the whole country against a possible Russian invasion. If that happened, Beijing was definitely a main target. Many organizations were ordered to move out of the city. Cadres and intellectuals were sent to do manual labor in so-called May 7 Cadre School in rural countries. The people left in the cities were urged to construct underground shelters for protection against possible nuclear attack. The population in the city diminished noticeably. Yeh noticed the surroundings were much quieter around his hostel.

The threat from the northern border might wake up the top level of CCP to the fact that dwelling on an internal power struggle and isolating the eight hundred million people from the rest of world was not the best thing for the country. Foreign dignitaries were invited one after another to visit Beijing. Many of them were from Africa and Eastern Europe. Pakistan was the Asian non-communist country that had good relations with PRC. Along with the news reports of Premier Zhou Enlai receiving so-and-so in the Great Hall of People, Yeh sometime read a paragraph or two describing how that foreign dignitary praised Mao's works.

These outreaching efforts did produce some results. Starting in 1970, many small countries formally recognized the People's Republic of China. Other countries that previously had no diplomatic relations set up ties with PRC. Even the United Kingdom and Japan came to negotiate on improving relations. To Yeh's surprise, an American capitalist, Edgar Snow, appeared by the side of Chairman Mao at Tiananmen to review the national anniversary parade. How could the CCP change its policy so rapidly? Even then the capitalist-roader was still regarded as a class enemy.

The fact that the Chinese team won the championship in the World Table Tennis Tournament held in Japan in April 1971 was a boost to the national pride in PRC. Then, when the American team was invited to visit China, everybody was surprised even more. The daily activities of this team were posted as headlines in the newspapers. Premier Zhou Enlai received the American table tennis team in the Great Hall of People on April 4 and said, "It is a new chapter in the relations of the American and Chinese people...."

"Does that mean that the CCP has given up anti-capitalist policy?" Yeh asked himself.

Nevertheless, the whole country caught "ping-pong fever." Even Zhu, the new cadre who replaced Cadre Yang a month earlier, came to ask Yeh whether he could play ping-pong.

Late one afternoon, Cadre Zhu led Yeh through the other door of the living room and into a room at the other end of the hallway. A ping-pong table was sitting in the middle of the room. Yeh had never been in this part of the house. He did not care to know who was using these rooms in the other side of the house, or how long the ping-pong table was there for what purpose. He enjoyed the game very much. Although he had not played ping-pong since his high school years, he was still a good match for Zhu. He had not had any real exercise for so many years, except some calisthenics. Ping-pong gave him the sensational feeling of panting and perspiration. Cadre Zhu enjoyed it too. He told Yeh he would come every other day if he had time. From that time on, ping-pong was the only thing that made Yeh forget he was in a jailhouse.

October first is the National Day of the People's Republic of China. The whole country had celebrated this holiday since 1949. There was always a spectacular parade held in front of Tiananmen and reviewed by the prominent Party members. As the date approached, the newspapers would always report what was to be seen in that parade or what other activities would be organized. To Yeh's surprise, it was very quiet in this late September of 1971. One day Cadre Zhu came to demand that Yeh handed over his little red book and tore out the preface of that book immediately, which was written by Lin Biao. He told Yeh, "We finally found out that Lin Biao is the real enemy of the country. Lin Biao plotted to assassinate Chairman Mao. We are fortunate the plot has failed."

Yeh later learned that Lin Biao had secretly organized a group of military officers in the name of "571" in March 1971 intending to overthrow Mao. Other officers loyal to Mao discovered the plot. Lin tried to escape by airplane on September 13. The airplane crashed in Mongolia. All on board were killed.

There must be a thorough investigation going on in the PLA to root out all the Lin's followers. Zhu did not come to play ping-pong anymore. Nor was any celebration held in China on October first 1971.

A week after National Day, Kuo came to tell Yeh, "Higher authority has decided that you can be released now. We are going to transfer you to a commune to learn more about the Proletarian Revolution from the peasants."

"But General Liu Yalou said that after the investigation of my case is completed I can go back to Taiwan," Yeh replied.

"Don't ever mention General Liu again. You know Liu used to be the general Chief of staff under Lin Biao."

"How long I am going to be in the commune?"

"I think it will probably be a year. One thing I would like to warn you is that you should never tell anybody that you were a U-2 pilot. It is for your own good. We will only tell the cadre there you were a captured KMT military officer and were released from prison recently. From now on your name is Yeh Changsheng."

Chapter Four: Reeducation

A few days later, Cadre Zhu came in the morning to tell Yeh to pack his belongings and to be ready to catch a train that afternoon. He said:

"You had better take all that you have now with you, including everything on the bed. The people in the commune are poor. You will not be able to buy a comforter there."

Yeh then asked Cadre Zhu for a hemp cord. He spread the comforter over the blanket, put all the belongings on them, wrapped with the comforter and then the blanket, and tied it with the cord. Life was simple. It did not take long to finish the packing. However, when he found that he had left the red-jacketed *Chairman Mao's Selected Works* on the table, he immediately unpacked the luggage and put the book in. It was the Bible of Chinese communism. How dare Yeh neglect it?

October is the most beautiful season in Beijing. A crisp wind blows away the smog in the city. Bright sunshine makes the leaves of trees even more colorful. Yeh sat on the chair and watched the scenery outside of the window. He had been watching the same scenery for countless days. Sometimes it was covered with snow. Sometimes it was veiled by heavy rain. Sometimes it was spotted with tender, green leaves. He had never appreciated the scenery so much as what was now in front of his eyes. The monotony of confined life made him insensitive to the surroundings. But it was now the time to leave this place. He might never have the opportunity to see it again. He felt somewhat nostalgic.

A black minivan came to take him to the train station. He carried his luggage to board the van. Cadre Zhu and the two soldiers all carried their own small bags and entered the minivan too. He understood that all three of them would accompany him to the commune and the journey might have to take more than one day. He asked Cadre Zhu:

"Where is the commune?"

"We are taking you to the Red Flag Commune. It is located at the southwest of Wuhan."

Being a U-2 pilot, Yeh certainly knew where Wuhan was. It is on the bank of the Yangtze River, the longest river in China, halfway between Chongqing, the capital of China during World War II, and Shanghai, the largest seaport of China. It was more than 2,000 kilometers from Beijing.

"It is going to be a long journey. It may take two days to get there by train. Hopefully, the train will have no delay along the way," Yeh said to himself.

The train station was huge, but still too small to accommodate the crowd of passengers. Cadre Zhu went through the noisy, cigarette-smoking crowds to a counter especially for military personnel to get the tickets. Then they proceeded to the platform.

There were already passengers swarming over the platform, pushing and shouting, trying to squeeze though the narrow gate of the train coach along with their luggage. The military uniform might have shown their authority, or the pistols hanging on the belts of soldiers' waists might have shown their power; there was no objection on the part of any person to giving way to Cadre Zhu's group to board the train.

Their seats were assigned in the middle section of a coach. By the time they boarded the train, all the seats in the coach were almost all filled. The overhead luggage racks were already packed to the ceiling. When they arrived at their booth, four men already had taken the seats. One of soldiers immediately yelled at them:

"Hey! Hey! You all get out of here. These are our seats."

These four men stood up right away and left, without any argument. They must have bought the tickets without seat reservations, or even had sneaked onto the train without tickets. The soldier told the men not to leave any of their bags on the racks over the seats. One of the men wearing an eight-cornered cap, which was commonly worn by old Communists in the 1930s, found an unoccupied seat just a few rows away from them. The rest of the men walked to the next coach.

Passengers kept boarding the train. Many of them laid their baggage on the aisle against seats. Some of them stood. Some squatted. Some sat on their bags or sat on the floor leaning against their bags. A teenager came up and stopped in front of that man wearing a Mao hat. He said politely:

"*Lao Bo* (老伯, old uncle), you have taken my seat."

"What you did you say?" The old man pretended not understanding the problem.

"This is my seat. You have taken my seat. Here is my ticket."

"It means nothing. I was here first."

"You see the number on my ticket. This is my seat. I have a long way to go," the teenager insisted.

"Young man, don't you respect seniors? Standing is good for you. I will let you have this seat when I arrive at my destination."

"Where is your destination?"

"Boading."

"That is more than three hours away."

The man smirked at the kid who must have been traveling for the first time all by himself. He did not know how to overcome this difficulty. Physically he was no match for the man in front of him. He pleaded so desperately, almost crying. The two men sitting on the opposite side of the booth seemed to have sympathy for the kid and said something to support him. The man wearing Mao hat finally moved a little bit to his right to press the old lady on his right side against the window walls, thus leaving about half a seat space on the kid's side. He pointed at the space and said to the kid:

"Don't fuss anymore. Sit down here."

Passengers kept coming and jammed the aisle until no one could walk through. The whistle finally blew and the train started to move. Yeh leaned against the windowsill and watched the houses and then the harvested wheat fields passing by. The rhythmic noise of train made him remember many of the journeys he had made with Betty, traveling by train to Taipei and back to Hsinchu while they were still dating. They both enjoyed the friendship, and felt fortunate to have found the right person to be in each other's company for the rest of their lives. Although those sentimental moments had taken place more than ten years ago, he could still remember many of the details. He treasured very much this memory. Kuo had told him that he would be freed after one year of reeducation in the commune. It was a promise to him. A promise was much better than no promise when he was incarcerated. Every mile the train raced forward seemed to bring him a bit closer to the day when he would reunite with Betty.

Along with the sun setting in the west, the scenery outside the window became hazier, until nothing could be distinguished. Most of the passengers had fallen asleep with their heads nodding with the rocking of the train. Yeh could not tell how many times he was awakened with a jerk, which happened when the train arrived or left a station. But this station was noisier than those previous ones. It must be a larger station.

Many passengers started moving toward the gates at both ends of the coach. Some vendors wearing white shirts and pushing wheeled carts along the platform outside of the windows shouted:

"Dinner, dinner, thirty cents a box!"

The windows on the platform side of the train were opened almost at the same time. Passengers stuck their heads out and waved with money in their hands to attract the vendors' attention. Cadre Zhu took out one RNB and twenty cents and told the soldier at the window to buy four meal boxes. Inside the box there was a steamed bun, a small piece of meat with fat and skin on it, and a few pickles. All the hungry mouths on the train welcomed it.

"The taste is good. But it isn't worth the money," one soldier commented.

"These are provided by the railroad. There are cheaper ones around. But the quality varies very much. Sometimes the vendors even take the money and give you an empty box or run away. You don't have time to go out of the train to argue with them," Cadre Zhu explained knowingly.

Cadre Zhu was right. A few minutes later, an old man at several booths away yelled at the vendor repeatedly, "Hey! Give me back the change."

The vendor continued walking away from the train without saying anything and soon disappeared in the shadow of the station. The train started to move. The old man was so disappointed and said to the people around him, "It is really a robbery!"

As the train left the lighted area of the station, people lost interest in looking out the window. The same atmosphere inside the coach came back. One soldier wanted to go to the bathroom. He had to prop his body up by his arms on wooden seat backs to let his foot find a tiny space on the floor, or step on someone's bag for walking through the packed aisle to the toilet. A moment later, he came back and said:

"There is no way to relieve myself in the toilet. It is also packed with people. I think I have to wait until the next station."

"I think I will go to the bathroom at the next station too," Yeh followed.

"*Lao* Yeh, I think you are not stupid enough to plan escaping by taking advantage of the darkness." Cadre Zhu spoke the words like teasing. But Yeh denied it seriously. Then Cadre Zhu continued:

"Even if you escape successfully, you have no money to buy food. Even if you have money, you don't have a government-issued food ticket. No one would sell you food without this food ticket.

Besides, your southern accent will show that you are a stranger in town. People will report you to the police immediately. You will be caught and sent back to us."

The train stopped at a shabby station with only one electrical light for the whole platform. The soldier opened the window and climbed out. Yeh followed him. Cadre Chu told the other soldier to follow Yeh.

The latrine was just several holes in the ground. The partitions between holes must have been taken away or stolen. The smell was awful. It looked like the place had never been cleaned in its existence. Under a dim light one could not tell whether there was mud, or urine, or feces on the ground. "What a relief!" Yeh said to himself when he came out of the latrine.

Before the train whistle blew again, they all clambered back into the train.

As the train was going south, the flat wheat fields outside of the window were gradually replaced by terraced rice paddies on the hillside, and then became wide-open areas again. They arrived at Wuhan on the second morning. A bus took them to the Red Flag Commune in one and a half hours.

Two men met them at the bus station. The man in a blue Mao jacket must have been a cadre. The other, a well-built man of middle age wearing a patched dress, introduced himself as Huang, a village leader of Red Army production brigade.

After Cadre Zhu finished some paperwork with these two men, he gave Yeh one hundred and twenty-some RMB, which he said was Yeh's balance of savings. It was quite a pleasant surprise to Yeh, although he knew the PLA Air Force provided him six RMB a month as allowance while he was incarcerated in the hostel. The cadre in the hostel kept the money to pay for his expenses and had never given Yeh a statement of how much the balance remained in his account these many years. Yeh had never asked how much money had been spent and how much he had saved.

Yeh put the money in his pocket like he had won a lottery.

Yeh loaded his luggage on the back rack of Huang's bicycle and followed him walking to the village. The cadre said that he had to attend another meeting and pedaled his own bicycle away. It was a winding country road in between the rice paddies. Huang soon let Yeh push his bicycle and walked by his side. After Huang understood that Yeh had never had any experience on a farm, he started to tell him about life in his village and what Yeh was supposed to do there.

The village had more than forty households, about one hundred adults. They were responsible for the land around the village and planted three crops a year, i.e., two crops of rice and one crop of wheat or rape. It was about time to harvest the second crop of the year. Yeh noticed some of the ears of grain on both sides of the road had become brownish.

All the members of the commune were required to meet in the open area in front of the house to pay respect to Chairman Mao and listen to Communist Party announcements every morning. Then they started their assigned work after the meeting and worked until dusk. From time to time, there would be meetings in the evening to discuss the work points, to complain of grievances or offer self-criticism, and to listen to the cadre sent by the Propaganda Department, who taught communist indoctrination.

In the commune, each member was rationed a certain amount of grain, salt, oil, and vegetables based on gender and age. Huang would lead Yeh to the village warehouse to receive the ration right after they had dropped his luggage off in Yeh's assigned living place. He would have a day off to settle down, and then join other team members to follow the daily schedule thereafter.

Having walked about an hour, the village finally appeared in the dim dusk light. There was a big house in the center of the village with many small mud-brick and thatch houses scattered around. Huang told him that the big house was property of a landlord, later confiscated by the Communist Party. Seven families now shared it. He would be another tenant of the house.

Yeh's room was at the left corner of the big house. Judging based on the small window high up on the wall, this room must have been a storage room before. A wooden board laid on two brick stacks was the bed. A table with three legs was leaning against the walls at a corner of the room. Huang introduced a woman of about sixty-some years old to Yeh as his next-door neighbor.

"*Lao Taitai* (老太太, a respectful address to an old lady), I am going to learn from you," Yeh greeted her humbly.

"Young man, you have got a lot to learn," she replied with authority. Yeh later learned that her husband died in the war against the KMT and her son died in the Korean War against the Americans. So she was classified as "red" and entitled to have some privilege in this village. She was illiterate but talked like a Communist, with indoctrinations frequently. She was now the leader of the women's team.

Lao Taitai was right! Yeh really had a lot to learn. From that time on, he had to take care of his own daily meals. He had never cooked a dish in all his life. Cooking would be the first lesson he had to learn in this "learning from peasants" reeducation. *Lao Taitai* told him how and where to buy some simple cooking utensils. She taught him every basic step of cooking. She even had to teach him that hissing of the kettle does not mean the water inside has reached the boiling temperature, and told him never to drink any water that had not been boiled. She taught him how to cook some vegetable dishes like a mother nurturing her son. Cooking oil was rationed, two ounces per month per person. She taught him how to cook with a minimum amount of oil for the dishes. Meat, poultry, and fish were only available on certain days of the week in a store about thirty minutes' walking distance away. Peasants had to get up very early in the morning to line up at the store and use their own money along with the commune-issued meat tickets to buy it. Each time Yeh had a chance to buy that scarce food, he always shared some with *Lao Taitai* to show his appreciation.

There was also a shortage of daily necessities. The commune issued each person a one-foot cloth ticket per month. Besides using it to buy towels or underwear, peasants had to save more than two years to buy a complete Mao suit. Almost all the peasants only bought pieces of cloth to patch their torn clothes. Yeh could not find anybody in the neighborhood wearing clothes without patches, unless someone was a cadre or secretary of the Communist Party. There was no toilet paper available, even to people willing to spend money on it. Fortunately, the Communist Party always provided newspaper everyday, which made a good substitute.

Yeh's first assignment was to follow the women's team, cultivate the vegetables, feed the livestock, and clean the barn and some public places. About a week after arriving at the commune and beginning his work, Yeh suddenly felt pain in his abdomen in the evening, followed by diarrhea. He might have eaten some spoiled food or have drunk contaminated water. He had to rush to the latrine repeatedly. The latrine was a big rectangular pit in the ground that served as storage for human excrement. A small straw hut covered a part of the big pit. Inside the hut, two long wooden bars placed about a foot apart over the pit allowed one to squat for relieving himself. It was a very miserable situation for him to walk about fifty meters back and forth on a narrow path between rice paddies to the latrine in the darkness and worry about mistakenly stepping into the rice paddy, or even the big hole full of manure.

The next morning, he felt too weak to work. *Lao Taitai* let him stay in his room for a day, and reminded him that he would lose eight work points. Every man would have ten work points for a day's work. Women were credited eight work points a day. The work points were used to calculate wages. At the year's end the commune would deduct the expenses of rations and monthly allowance from the peasant's wage and pay the rest in cash. If someone did not accumulate enough work points, he must pay back the deficit. Yeh fasted a whole day to stop the diarrhea.

Yeh was ordered to join the men's team when the harvest of the second crop of the year started. Huang allocated the jobs for all the team members. There were no machines. Hoes, harrows, and sickles were the only metal tools available. Farmers cut the stalks of rice with sickles. They held a bundle of stalks and swung their husks overhead to strike the wood bars over a box to thresh the grains from their stems. They used shoulder poles to carry heavy loads. All the work was done manually. Communists had not made any improvement these many years. Yeh was always exhausted when the team leader announced a day's work was done.

During the planting season, the water buffalo helped plow the field. Yet to hold the plowshare at the right position needed skill and strength. Yeh spent a great deal of effort learning how to control both the buffalo and the plowshare. Bending down to transplant the rice seedlings was even more difficult to endure. Yeh almost could not straighten his back again after a few hours' labor. Standing in the water-covered mud also provided a good opportunity for leeches to feast on workers. It was not uncommon to see several blood-sucking leeches hanging onto a peasant's calves and bare feet when he stepped out of the muddy water. It was another lesson that Yeh had to learn from the peasants: how to remove those greedy leaches from his legs.

Between planting and harvest, there was not much work to do except irrigation and weeding in the rice fields for about two months. The team then would be dispatched to build a road or to construct a dam. There seemed never to be time for them to rest all year round. Yeh understood that he had been sent to the commune to be reeducated, as a kind of punishment. He could not understand why all these peasants had to be treated the same punishment.

One day, he found there was another bed in his room when he came back from the field. Soon an old man came in and introduced himself as Qin. He had just been released from a prison. His slow and frail motion showed he had been malnourished for a long time. He wore a white armband with black characters, "Counterrevolutionary" (反革命). Counterrevolutionary was one of the five "black" categories (黑五類), which included: landlords, rich peasants, counterrevolutionaries, bad elements, and rightists. Peasants were taught to hate the "blacks" and treat them badly. "Mercy on the class enemy is unfair to the masses."

Huang assigned Qin to collect human and animal excrement around the commune and from the nearby towns, which was regarded as the most despicable job in the commune. He usually carried two wooden barrels, a bamboo shoulder pole, and a long ladle, leaving for his daily journey after the morning meeting and coming back at dusk. The weary expression on his face revealed he had worked all he could that day. Qin was also assigned to fertilize the planted vegetables with diluted excrement from time to time. Yet he could only earn seven work points every hard-working day. Even so, when Party Secretaries of various levels of the commune presided over the evening meetings, some of the peasants still criticized Qin for not doing a good job, to show their practice of Mao's teaching. After Qin earnestly requested many times, the Party Secretary finally allowed him to cease wearing the white armband every day.

Qin was a quiet man. Yeh was happy to have Qin as his roommate and to have him to share the cooking. Unfortunately, Qin snored loudly, which often woke Yeh up in the middle of the night, and then he had difficulty getting to sleep again. Yeh always felt lousy the following day for lack of sleep. When the barefoot doctor came he asked for help. The doctor gave him some sleeping pills. The pills did give him a sound sleep.

Barefoot doctor was a special professional in Communist China. They did not have any formal training in medicine. They were provided with a "manual" and told to follow the manual to help sick people in rural areas. Shoes were expensive, and the doctor had to carry his medicine case and walk from village to village barefoot. That was probably how the name "barefoot doctor" was coined.

The doctor was scheduled to visit Yeh's village every other week. But he rarely came on time. So Yeh always asked the doctor to give him as many pills as permitted, no matter whether the doctor came earlier than the scheduled date or not. On the other hand, Yeh refrained from taking sleeping pills regularly to avoid becoming addicted. He saved the remaining pills in the bottle in case the doctor did not show up for a long time.

One evening there was no meeting and the sky was covered with low clouds and drizzle; both Yeh and Qin had no place to go. They lay down on their beds and watched the tiles of the thin roof lighted by the dim tung oil lamp. After Qin got to know that Yeh was a captured KMT officer, he gradually told Yeh about his past.

He was brought up in a rural country about 150 kilometers west of Wuhan. His grandfather was a tenant farmer. But his father worked very hard to save some money to buy land, one plot after another. When Qin was in grade school, he had to help his parents in the field after school, until he was sent to a high school in town. By the time he was in university in Wuhan, his parents were doing quite well. They could afford to hire several laborers to help manage their farm.

Qin worked for the government after graduation. When the Communists defeated the KMT and the economy in China was disastrous, he did not follow the KMT to Taiwan. He hoped the new government would change the economic situation. He found a job in a high school in Wuhan as a mathematics teacher. Life was not prosperous, yet the government rationed enough food and clothes. He then married a clerk in the same school.

Not long after his parents came to his house to participate in their first grandson's one-month-old banquet, the land reform started in the rural country around Wuhan. All the landlords were forced to give up their properties. Then the Communists classified Qin's parents as rich peasants. They were only allowed to keep a small portion of their own farmland. The rest was redistributed to poor farmers. Their house had to be equally shared with four other families. Every time Qin went back to visit his parents, he found there was no way to comfort their resentment and sorrow. They could not tolerate seeing the accomplishments of life-long endeavor stripped away without any form of compensation.

A few years later, Mao announced a policy known as the "Let a hundred flowers bloom and a hundred thoughts contend" (百花齊放), which meant greater freedom of speech. People were encouraged to criticize officials. All the intellectuals were excited, as they traditionally liked to impress others with their unique opinions. Qin criticized the injustice of indiscriminately confiscating rich farmer's property. Many of them, like his parents, had never exploited any others to build their wealth. There was no sense in redistributing the property of an industrious and capable person to lazy and ignorant beggars.

The cadres in school soon denounced his opinion as having "bourgeois reactionary" thinking. It was not difficult for him to defend himself against those poor, educated cadres in many struggle meetings. But he was soon named as a "rightist." In addition, he had worked for the KMT government for a couple years; he was sentenced to learn Mao's ideology thoroughly.

In the spring of 1958, he followed a group of "rightists" to arrive at "Great Northern Wilderness" (北大荒), which was a huge Communist labor camp for political prisoners located at the northeast border of China near Lake Khanka. The weather was harsh, work hours were long, and food was scarce. After five years of "reeducation," Qin was released back to his school. He found his parents all had died, his wife often complained that his status caused her trouble, and his boy respected Chairman Mao more than his own parents, especially his father. Qin understood their awkward situation. Once you were classified as "black," your whole family also became "black." Even your grandson would be labeled as being from a "black" family. His son had to show himself more like a Communist than the Communists.

Even though he had learned from the labor camp to speak like a Communist, the Cultural Revolution did not spare him. This time he was accused of being a spy for the American imperialists. Someone under torture confessed that he had worked voluntarily for an American missionary for a short period in the early 1950s. He also mentioned Qin's name in the long list of people presented in some Sunday worships. To the Red Guards, all the foreigners were regarded as suspected spies.

Qin was put into prison and coaxed to confess what secrets he had passed to this American "spy." After so many years, he could hardly remember he had ever had any personal contact with that American missionary. What could he confess? Torture often was followed by no satisfactory answer. He was then classified as a "counterrevolutionary." His wife severed their relationship. His boy disappeared in the crowd of Red Guards.

Time in prison had no meaning. Qin could not tell how long he had been incarcerated, until the announcement that President Nixon would visit China in May 1972, which might change the Communists' policy toward American missionaries. Qin's confession had lost its importance. He was then released to this commune.

Qin continued his comments:

"... The Chinese name of Communist Party (共產黨) means the Party advocates 'equally sharing resources among the masses.' People believed that in the very beginning. But, you know, all the Party members receive better pay than the populace. Even within the public services, there are twenty-six grades of different salaries and fringe benefits, including clothing, housing, and transportation. When we were in Great North Waste Land, we were almost starved to death. The officials were still wining and dining in their hostel every day....

"... The Communists helped the tenant farmers to prosecute the landlords. Now the Communist Party became the sole landlord. In the old days the landlord might collect 30 percent of the produce from the tenant farmer. The Communist Party only lets the farmer have barely enough to live and takes all the rest away. Don't you see? We raise pigs, chickens, and ducks, and they, in the name of so-called 'planned economy,' take them all away. We have to buy them with meat tickets. They are much worse than landlords....

"... The Communists never let you live in peace. Don't you know how many movements had been conducted since 1949? Each movement made some unfortunate ones miserable. The 'blacks', like us, are always the easy targets. I don't know when the next movement will be....

"... Many years ago, the warlord might rob your belongings. The Communists now control all your life. They make people spy on each other closely. People don't have privacy in this country; don't even have the right to remain silent....

"... They are against religion, but they ask people to confess, ask people to repent, like Catholics do. For the Catholics, one kneels down in the confessional to confess to the priest behind the screen, who represents God to forgive his sin. He doesn't have to let the priest recognize him. He can be sure that the priest will not let anyone know what he had said. The Communists ask people to confess in front of the masses even they had done nothing wrong. What a person has confessed will burden him for the rest of his life...."

From Qin's story, Yeh understood that Qin was about his senior by ten years. But Qin looked so old. The prison life must have destroyed his health.

It was a market day. Yeh went to the store and lined up with the crowd to buy some meat. But the meat was all sold out just a few peasants in front of him. He browsed around and found plenty of cigarettes on the shelf behind the counter. He asked the salesgirl which brand was the best and bought a carton of them.

Not long after he came to the commune, Huang asked him to lend some money to buy cigarettes, for he had spent all his money to entertain Party Secretaries of Red Flag Commune. From that time on, Huang asked to borrow money several times and never mentioned paying it back. On the other hand, he realized Huang gradually treated him better, allocating less strenuous jobs for him, raising his work points to ten a day, assigning him to read the newspaper article in the morning meeting, etc. He was not sure this had any relation with lending money. Anyway, a carton of good cigarettes as a gift would please Huang a lot.

The summer in Wuhan area is steamy hot. The old man in charge of the village warehouse died. Huang recommended to the Party secretary that Yeh take over the job of managing the warehouse, as he was probably the only educated man, besides Qin, in the village who was able to count and to record the food distribution. He then moved to live in the warehouse.

The warehouse room was much larger. The grains, oil, and many kinds of daily necessities piled up on one side of the room and on the shelves hanging on the wall. A single bed, a desk, and a chair lay on the other side. There was an abacus on the desk, which he had not any chance to use since grade school. It seemed he had to master it by practicing, as he could only remember some simple rules of adding and subtracting.

The warehouse keeper only had to work half a day in the field. He could relax in his room after lunch. At the same time he realized the peasants seemed to greet him more politely, which he understood, because the peasants did not want him to mess up their food ration records, either unintentionally or intentionally. The peasants were mostly illiterate and not able to keep their own records.

September was the happiest month in the commune. The peasants had been working very hard under the hot sunshine for quite some time to harvest the first rice crop, plow the paddies, and then transplant the tender rice shoots of the second crop. Especially the backbreaking labor of cutting rice stalks with sickle and inserting rice seedlings on the muddy field brought everybody, including the born farmer, nearly to collapse at the end of the day's assignment. The task that followed was weeding, which required kneeling down on the muddy field covered with shallow water to root out weeds by hand. It would not take much time and strength as the others. Late afternoon thunderstorms occasionally cooled off the steamy weather a bit. Peasants were looking forward to the Mid-Autumn Festival.

At one evening meeting, Huang told Yeh that Kuo would like to see him the next day. He was supposed to meet Kuo at the bus station in the morning. It was good news to Yeh, as he thought Kuo was the only authority he knew in charge of his fate. One-year reeducation in the rural country, as Kuo told him, was almost completed. Kuo might come to tell him that he would be released to Taiwan soon. He was very excited and did not get much sleep, only happy dreams.

He got up very early the next morning and ate a full bowl of rice, the leftovers of the evening meal the night before, with some pickles. He started to walk to leave the village in the early light of dawn, though the meeting would not be until around ten o'clock. It only took him about an hour to reach the station. He just could not wait in his room.

The bus station was at the edge of a small town. A store beside the station was about to open. Some bottled water, cigarettes, and confectionaries were on the shelves behind the counter in the store, and several tables and chairs occupied the area outside of the counter. Yeh went in and sat on a chair. The shopkeeper told him they did not have boiled water yet if Yeh wanted to have a cup of tea. Yeh did not mind. He just liked to have a place to sit and wait.

Some people started to show up in the bus station. The buses came and went about every half an hour, both ways. As each bus came, Yeh walked close to the bus and carefully watched every person get down from the bus, and even he knew that Kuo could not arrive until around ten o'clock.

Kuo finally came, followed by three junior officers.

"*Lao* Kuo, long time no see you (好久不見). What wind brings you here?"

"We came down to this area to inspect the subordinate organizations."

They came into the store. Yeh ordered tea and some biscuits for the guests. He noticed there was another star on each of the collar patches of Kuo's uniform.

"You must have had another promotion, *Lao* Kuo. Congratulations!"

"That means more responsibility, more headaches, and less leisure time. *Lao* Yeh, How about you?"

Yeh told them about life in the commune and that he had recently taken over the responsibility of managing the village warehouse. Kuo told him about what the cadres had been doing, those cadres he knew during the years Yeh had been confined in the hostel. At one point Kuo mentioned the changes that had been made after President Nixon's visit, which caused the other three officers to speak their feelings. They were so proud of Chairman Mao's prestige that made the president of the most powerful nation of the world fly half a globe to beg for an audience with Chairman Mao.

Yeh understood Kuo's team was on the way from Wuhan to Yueyang. They could go there by train; instead, they came by bus in order to make a stop for Kuo to see Yeh. Yeh appreciated this very much. They were supposed to catch the next bus to leave in thirty minutes. As the time passed fast when people strive to express themselves, Yeh could not wait more and asked:

"*Lao* Kuo, when will I be released from the commune?"

"I haven't heard anything about this from higher authority yet."

"I remember you said before I left from Beijing that I would be released in about one year. It is almost a year now."

"*Lao* Yeh, I think you have to be patient."

"You know I have a wife and parents in Taiwan. We have been separated for almost nine years now. I miss them so much. Could you ask your superiors to consider my case?"

"I will do that. But for your information, your wife has remarried."

What Kuo had said! Yeh could not believe what he had heard. On the way back, Yeh seemed to walk in a dense fog. His body was controlled completely by his subconscious. His brain was occupied with repeated questions. Had Betty forgot our vow, "Till death do us part"? Had the Republic of China Air Force changed his status from "missing in action" to "killed in action"? Did Kuo bluff to discourage him? *What will I do without Betty?* He wandered along the muddy ridges between paddy fields. He rested on the rubble under a tree sometimes. He just did not want to meet anybody before he could find any reasonable answer.

The sun went down to the western horizon. He dragged his feet stepping into his warehouse room and closed the door immediately. He felt hungry, but did not have the mood to prepare any food. He took from his pocket the leftover biscuits of what he bought for Kuo's team, and swallowed them all at once with some water.

He lay down on his bed. The mosquitoes hummed around. He unfolded the mosquito net to cover his bed. The Indian summer made the temperature inside the mosquito net even more unbearable. But he did not make any moves. The questions kept hammering his brain.

"There were many times in the past eight years he had felt so desperate and could not stand the solitary anymore; the thought that Betty was waiting for him in Taiwan was always the trigger to overcome his depression. But Betty is now in someone's arms. What would his life be without Betty?

"The life under the Communist regime is so intolerable. In addition to the poor living conditions and heavy workload, there is no freedom, no privacy, everyone watches over each other's shoulder, and no one dares to make any real friends. No one dares to stop worshiping Chairman Mao. No one dares to stop reciting Communist slogans. No one dares to say anything against, much less to criticize, Party members, the cadres, even the village leader. They are the emperors of the commune. They always take more than their allotted shares when they come to the warehouse to get their rations. I have no way to balance the books, unless I reduce the actual quantity for each peasant.

"Besides, 'There is no peace of life,' as Qin said. '**Black** is always the easy target of any political movement.' There is no law to follow. Everyone's fate is determined by the discretion of some uneducated people at some level of the Communist hierarchy. They had promised to release me to go back to Taiwan since the very beginning. All these years they had never denied their promise, but never gave me any date. All these are hopeless...."

The waxing moon was almost full. It moved out of clouds and cast its light through the window on the floor in front of Yeh's bed, which made Yeh realize it was already midnight. He still could not fall asleep. Taking a sleeping pill might relieve his distress. He got out of the bed and reached out for the bottle containing the pills in the drawer of the desk, which he had not touched since he moved to this warehouse room. It was a full bottle of sleeping pills. A caprice caught him suddenly. "A pill may eliminate his vexation for a night, then I have to face those unanswered questions again. Why not take the whole bottle of pills to solve all problems once and for all?"

He sat on the chair to contemplate. "If I die, there will not be much change in my parents' lives. I trust my brothers will continue to take care of them. They all live in Taiwan. If I die, Huang might face some difficulty, as he was assigned to supervise my reeducation. Huang has been treating me fairly well. But I cannot continue to endure suffering just because of him. At least, I should write a letter to state he had not any involvement in my suicide. I should list clearly all the records of receiving and distribution of the stocks in the warehouse, so someone would not have difficulty in taking over my job."

He lit the lamp and started to write the last letter of his life. "… Insomnia bothered me continuously, which made me lose all my will to live. I regard myself as having no use to the Communist Party. I had better leave this world and not waste any more food of the masses..… I have a small amount of money in my pocket. Please buy cigarettes for Huang, the great village leader.…"

He swallowed all the pills with water and then lay down on the bed. He felt tranquil as he completed the most important duty of his life. Nothing would bother him anymore!

Lost Black Cats

Young Lovers 1958.
Betty and Yeh.

ROC RF-101 Pilots: Yeh (*second from right, back row*) and Lee Nanping (*second from right, front row*) were later flying U-2s and were shot down by ChiCom SA-2 missiles.

Yeh showed Generalissimo Chiang Keishek the RF-101 he flew and brought back clear pictures of five new enemy airfields on the other side of Taiwan Strait, 1961.

Yeh's First Wedding 1962.
Back row from left: Yeh's mother and father,
Betty's mother and father.

Lost Black Cats

Generalissimo Chiang Kaishek, in the president's office, summoned Major Yeh after a successful U-2 mission in 1963.

Chapter Five: New Hope

As the morning stars gave way to the bright sun, the peasants walked slowly from their homes to assemble in the open area in front of the large house for the morning ritual. Male peasants gathered on the right side, females on the left, facing Chairman Mao's portrait hanging on the wall on the opposite side of the house. Each one stood on his or her assigned position in the ranks and files, so the cadre could easily spot who was absent or late.

Huang brought the *People's Daily* newspaper and came to the open area. He could not find Yeh in the crowd. Yeh was supposed to read the headline news and editorial to the peasants. After waiting for a few minutes, Yeh still had not shown up. Huang thought Yeh must have overslept. He went to the warehouse and called Yeh's name several times, but no answer. He sensed there must be something wrong inside the room. He pushed the door open by force and found Yeh lying on the bed unconscious. Yeh's breath was very slow and weak. Huang held up his wrist and tried to check his heartbeat. The hand was cold and the pulse could hardly be detected. The empty bottle and the short letter on the desk told him Yeh had committed suicide. He rushed out to call the cadre for help.

They went back to Yeh's room and had a brief discussion. Then, Huang grasped Yeh's left wrist and left ankle, put Yeh on his back and started to walk toward the clinic. The cadre walked back to conduct the morning meeting.

The nearest clinic was about forty-five minutes' walking distance away. Huang carried Yeh all the way to the clinic without stopping for a rest, although he perspired and panted most of the journey. The movement of steps seemed a forced physical therapy to rhythmically help Yeh's breath and circulation.

There was only a nurse available in the clinic. She asked Huang to place Yeh on a bench facing down and tried to induce vomiting by sticking a finger down his throat. Yeh did not show much response. Then a doctor rushed in and the nurse finally hooked up the intravenous feeding equipment, injecting some kind of medicine.

When Yeh opened his eyes several hours later, he felt so exhausted and his brain seemed to be not functioning. With the blurred vision, he did not have any interest in finding out where he was, whether he was still in the mortal world or in heaven. He only recognized this was a place he had never been before. Not until the nurse came into the room and told him she was happy about having saved his life, he understood that his suicide attempt had failed. He was very disappointed. Then she said to him:

"Do you know that Huang carried you on his back and walked almost an hour from your village to here? You are really lucky to have a village leader as strong as he is. Otherwise you would never have woken up again."

Yeh had nothing to reply. He just questioned himself, "Am I really lucky?"

In the late afternoon, the nurse came to pull out the intravenous needle. Soon Qin showed up by the side of his bed. He brought with him a small pot of chicken noodle soup. The smell of the soup made Yeh feel hungry. Qin told him that rumor in the village spread very fast. The whole village got to know about his suicide just at the end of the morning meeting. Then the news that Yeh had been saved came around noontime. Then Qin said:

"*Lao* Yeh, I don't want to know what made you so desperate. Do you believe God has a plan for everybody? No one can change it by oneself. We can only try our best to glorify Him. I always regard you as a man of clear thinking. You must have your reason to end your life, but God has a plan for you. He led Huang to rescue you in such a difficult situation...."

These few sentences kept coming back to Yeh's mind after Qin had left for home. Yeh had never attended any church services since he had left Hong Kong. Even in Hong Kong he just occasionally went to the church on Sundays, to comply with a friend's earnest invitation. He almost had no idea of Christianity. Qin's words made him aware there might be a God; otherwise, he would not have survived in the first place after the SA-2 missile exploded near his U-2. He certainly would not survive this time either. "If God has a plan for me as Qin said, what is the plan?" The question appeared in Yeh's mind until he went to sleep again.

Next day, not long after he finished the rice porridge that the nurse provided, Huang came into the room.

"I am very glad to see you alive again, *Lao* Yeh. You look like you have almost completely recovered. Can you follow me to walk back to our village?"

Yeh had no objection as he realized there were several peasants already in the clinic and also lined up outside waiting to seek help from the nurse. As he did not wear shoes when Huang carried him to the clinic, Yeh had to walk back barefoot. He still felt very weak and dizzy. His whole body seemed still half asleep, especially his brain.

"*Lao* Yeh, you had scared me to death. You know if you had died I would be in big trouble. As I am responsible for your reeducation, committing suicide is regarded by the Party as an attempt to resist reeducation; I would certainly be condemned, and maybe punished to exile to a distant, poor commune away from my family. I don't believe the reason for killing yourself as you stated in you letter. Nobody will believe that either. For whatever the reason is, please don't do it again in my village...."

Huang was a plain rural man. He always spoke in a straightforward manner. Yeh had no reason to make him feel wretched. Yeh had no proper words to respond, except to apologize.

Lao Taitai came to see Yeh that afternoon. She brought some cooked food for him. After a few questions of asking about his health, she said:

"*Hsiao* Yeh, you look like a bright young man. How could you take such a shortsighted action? You have disappointed me! All the revolutionaries should fight against any obstacle until death, not give up before fighting."

Yeh did not go to work in the field the next few days. The peasants resumed coming to get their portion of rations. He noticed their attitude had changed. They wore impassive faces and offered no friendly greeting; business only to complete the transaction. They rushed away as soon as they got their share of food, like minimizing the contact with a pest.

The Party secretary of the Red Army Production Brigade came in the following evening meeting. Soon after he made a public address to express that it was fortunate Yeh's suicide attempt had not succeeded, one of peasants sitting in the front row stood up facing Yeh and said:

"Comrade Yeh, you have disgraced our Red Army Production Brigade. We had never had anyone in our brigade commit suicide. You have now smeared our remarkable record."

It was really a remarkable record, as Yeh understood. During the Red Guard era, numerous people committed suicide all over the country, unable to stand the humiliation and torture.

Many other peasants stood up one after another and said:

"Comrade Yeh, why don't you follow Chairman Mao's doctrine? Chairman Mao taught us, 'Suicide is a cowardly act. Only those who have no courage to fight for revolution, those who resist reform and reeducation, commit this crime.'"

"Comrade Yeh, you have betrayed the great Proletarian Revolution. We don't want any reactionary in our brigade. We ask Comrade Yeh to repent."

"… Crime…. Repent…." "… Coward…." "… Reactionary…."
"… Repent…."

It seemed the meeting would never end unless Yeh said something to compromise. Yeh was totally confused.

The next day, the Party secretary came to the village and said to Yeh:

"Comrade Yeh, I hope you don't have any bad feelings toward those comrades criticizing you last night. Chairman Mao taught us, '… In treating an ideological or a political malady, one must adopt the approach of curing the sickness, as a doctor cuts the diseased organ off to save his patient.' They are trying to save you. You should thank them for their kindness.

"Our Party has decided to transfer you to the commune tool factory to let you have a place to start a new life. Huang will take you there. It's a shame that your reeducation has to be extended for another three years."

It sounded like the pronouncement of sentence by a judge. However, it did not make Yeh more depressed. Some unknown authorities controlled his fate under the Communist regime. All their favorable promises had never been materialized. Just like the good prognosis by the doctor had never been realized, why should he worry about a bad prognosis?

In a late September morning of 1972, Yeh carried his baggage on his shoulder and walked alongside Huang to the commune tool factory. The factory was located on the outskirts of a town near the bus station. Inside the gate of brick walls a small hangar and a row of living quarters stood on both sides with an open space in between. A large portrait of Chairman Mao hung on the wall facing the gate. The factory Chief, Zheng, came to meet them and led Yeh to a room in the living quarters. There were two bunk beds, one table, and four stools. A rack at one corner held washbasins with a cup and toothbrush in each basin. An electrical bulb was mounted on the ceiling of the room. The living conditions looked better than that in the village.

Yeh noticed only one top bed was not occupied. He put his belongings on that bed. Zheng told him to start to work after lunch, which would be available in the dining room at one end of the same building.

The loudspeaker started to broadcast revolutionary songs. Yeh saw people walked out from the hangar to the dining room. It was the time to break for lunch. Yeh followed them. A young man about twenty-some years old came near to greet him:
"Comrade, you must be the newcomer. I am Pan. Chief Zheng told me that you are going to take the top level of my bunk bed."
"Comrade Pan, glad to meet you. My name is Yeh. You will have to teach me how to cope with life in this factory."

The dining room had two long tables with benches on both sides, which could hold about twenty people. There was a window on the wall next to the kitchen. People went there to get their shares of food to eat at the table. "The food is lousy, but I don't have to cook by myself," Yeh thought.

After lunch and a half an hour rest, Yeh followed Pan to the hangar. Yeh noticed there was a small lathe, a drilling machine, a grinder, and several benches with vises mounted on them, and many woodworking tools spread around. A pile of stock, from raw material to half-finished products, was piled in a corner of the hangar. Chief Zheng came to lead him to the place outside the hangar under the extended roof. There were a furnace and some manual forging tools lying around. Zheng introduced the blacksmith, Liang, to Yeh and told Yeh to follow Liang's order to help him. That afternoon, Yeh began to learn how to lift up a sledgehammer high and to pound the right point where Liang pointed with a small hammer on a red-hot iron rod laying over an anvil while Liang grasped the rod with long pliers and turned it around. They were making blanks of farming tools.

The day's work ended at dusk. Yeh followed the workers to the dining room again. Then he met the other two roommates, Sun and Jing. Several other workers living in other rooms greeted him too. Many of them, like Pan, were in their early twenties. Many of them spoke with northern accents. They might have joined the Red Guards in high school, gone through the turmoil of the Cultural Revolution, and then, after President Liu Shaoqi had been prosecuted, joined Chairman Mao's "Up to the Mountains, Down to the Countryside (上山下岡)" movement to be dispatched far away from home to this Red Flag Commune.

Pan told him that bachelor workers usually played cards in the dining room after dinner if there was no evening meeting, which was held regularly twice a week. He asked Yeh whether he knew how to play "Hundred Points." Yeh certainly knew how to play it. He had played that game many many times with other pilots when they were waiting for orders to fly a mission in the pilot's lounge of the Air Force squadrons in Taiwan. He was quite good at it. However, learning to handle a heavy sledgehammer properly the first afternoon in the factory had wearied him completely. He went back to his room.

The next morning the loudspeaker woke him up. He followed his roommates to go to the dining room to have breakfast, and then assembled in the open area to worship Mao and to listen to the headline news and the Communist indoctrination broadcast through the loudspeaker.

Factory work started at eight o'clock. All of them took long breaks after working for about two hours, sitting or squatting against the outside wall of the hangar, smoking cigarettes, drinking tea from flasks or tin mugs, telling jokes, teasing each other, gossiping, even playing simple chess on the ground until Chief Zheng or the Party secretary rushed them back to work again. No one seemed to have the drive to accomplish anything, because the work points were counted based on the rate of attendance, not on the job accomplished.

Life in the factory was like riding on a perpetual vehicle along with others. There was always someone accompanying you. There was no private time. After a good exercise of handling the sledgehammer, Yeh had always a good night's sleep. He had no time to think about his past or his future. Time passed without leaving any trace.

As the days went by, Yeh gradually got to know that Pan was a member of the Elite Youth League under the Communist Party. At the evening meeting, which mostly was presided over by the factory Party secretary, Pan always spoke the same language as the secretary. He sometimes postured as the deputy of the secretary. Yeh noticed when Pan came into the room, Sun and Jing often changed their topics of conversation immediately. He had better behave carefully in front of Pan. Pan must be responsible for monitoring him too.

When the weather was bearable, the evening meeting was held in the open area. People brought their own stools there. Many times a cadre from the Propaganda Department came to elaborate the Party's policies and orders, and to denounce someone's reactionary conduct. To Yeh's surprise, although it was already more than a year after Lin Biao's death, he was still being denounced for all the crimes he had committed since the days of Long March (the Communists' retreat in the 1930s, under the KMT's military pressure, from Central China to Yanan, the northern, hilly wilderness) and being officially designated as Chairman Mao's heir. It must be very difficult to convince the populace how a role model of Chairman Mao's follower, praised so much in the Cultural Revolution, could plot to kill Chairman and suddenly became the enemy of the masses.

Yeh had gradually learned that Liang, the blacksmith, was originally the owner of this factory. In the early 1950s in the name of "nationalization," the Communists confiscated his factory. Because he had stubbornly refused to cooperate, he was sent to a commune in Guizhou Province, the poorest country in southwest China. People described it as a place where "no clear sky lasts for three days, no flat land extends three feet, and no one owns three ounces of silver" (天無三日晴, 地無三尺平, 人無三兩銀). The factory then deteriorated continuously almost to the point where no quality products could be manufactured under the management of Party-selected personnel.

But the PRC's admission to the United Nations in late 1971 liberated the country from its self-imposed isolation away from developed countries for so many years, and made the government realize that technical skill are at least as important as political indoctrination. Liang was then called back to his lost factory. Besides taking the job as a blacksmith, he was also responsible for getting those machines in the hangar in good condition and teaching the workers how to operate them. He clearly understood it was not his factory anymore, yet he wanted to see the facility live up to its capability. He had, after all, invested it all his inheritance and had toiled in it for so many years. The factory was still his baby, although he did not concern himself with the productivity of the factory.

The "Up to the Mountains, Down to the Countryside" movement started in late 1968 did subdue the Red Guard's turmoil. However, the Cultural Revolution was still continuing. The CCP persistently campaigned against the "four olds"—old ideas, old customs, old culture, and old habits. They encouraged the children to denounce, even to beat, their parents. Filial piety of Confucian virtues was regarded as feudalism. But they could not change the custom of celebrating the Chinese New Year, even though no one worshiped his ancestors openly with specially prepared food and the burning of tin-coated paper money anymore. The farmers took a long vacation, wore clean clothes, visited relatives, or played dominoes. Gambling was not regarded as a vice during the New Year holidays. The people in town celebrated with rallies to praise Chairman Mao, along with dancing and singing.

At this time, the factory had a week's vacation. Some of the workers took leaves to visit their families. Yeh went with a few colleagues to the town center to watch the celebration. The red banners around the center square fluttered in the wind. The loudspeaker blasted the song "East is Red." People seemed never to get tired of repeating the song, like chanting Buddhist scriptures with the lyrics:

"East is red, the sun has risen.
China has born a Mao Zedong.

He works hard for the people.

Hu ya! Hai ya! He is the people's great savior" (大救星).

Many peasants stood around the square watching a group of others, young and old, wearing red scarves around their necks, linking arms, and following revolutionary music to do the loyalty dance: two steps in place, one step forward, then kick, kick. Yeh had seen that kind of celebration in Beijing not long after he was transferred there. Cadre Zhao took him to see a big rally to honor a high-ranking Party member. To his surprise, after so many years, singing the "East is red" and dancing the "loyalty dance" were still the only accepted ways to celebrate.

"There must be no one who dared to change it and no one was permitted to create anything new," Yeh thought.

The spring of 1973 brought the peach blossom season. Some of the rice fields had already been covered with rapeseed flowers. The pink peach blossom loosely spotted above the tender, yellow flowers on top of the green rapeseed leaves made a colorful picture under the bright morning sun. The radio broadcast news announced that Deng Xiaoping has been rehabilitated to be the vice premier again. He had been the vice premier for many years until the revolt of the Red Guards. He had been prosecuted as a "capitalist-roader" and banished from his post to a remote factory then. His rehabilitation indicated that there might be some change in the political climate.

After the People's Republic of China was admitted to the United Nations at the end of 1971, many countries established normal relations with PRC. Many countries sent official representatives to the PRC and also sent business specialists to explore the market potential of one billion people. The PRC also sent representatives to other countries to participate in international activities. People gradually realized that the living standards in the PRC were far behind the other countries. It became obvious that economic improvement could not be achieved by practicing only the Cultural Revolution led by Chairman Mao's wife, Jiang Qing. Some experienced technocrats had to be appointed in the government.

A few months later, Pan came to ask Yeh for help:

"*Lao* Yeh, would you mind helping me study? I was told the universities would reopen this fall. They are going to recruit students from young workers, farmers, and soldiers through open-entrance examinations. I should not miss this good opportunity. Unfortunately, I joined the Red Guards at my first year of high school and I have never touched any books except official Communist publications in the past seven years. I know I have a lot to catch up on. Would you please teach me?"

"How do you know I have the capability to teach you?" Yeh replied.

"I know you were a KMT officer. You must have graduated from high school before you entered the KMT military academy."

Yeh remembered Pan was a member of the Communist Youth League. He must have a way to access Yeh's dossier. In the PRC, every adult had a dossier (檔案), which recorded his personal life, any activities he participated in, and any words he said, especially those related to Chairman Mao's teaching. The person was never allowed to see it. He should never know what was in it. He could never know whether there were false accusations in that file. It followed each person wherever he went. That made the office that controlled the personnel dossiers very powerful. During the Red Guard revolt, the students raided class enemies' homes and denounced them in the struggle meetings, all based on the information recorded in the dossiers released to them by the Party. The factory Party secretary must control Yeh's dossier. He knew the Party secretary liked Pan very much.

Yeh agreed to help Pan. The entrance examination would cover the subjects of the Chinese language, politics, math, chemistry, and physics. Yeh promised to help him for the last three subjects. He told Pan to find the high school textbooks of those subjects. From that time on, Yeh became Pan's private tutor.

In one evening, when Pan was not in the room, Yeh asked Sun and Jing why they did not follow Pan to prepare for college entrance examination. Their reply was that only politically qualified candidates could take the college entrance examination. They did not have slightest chance to go through the screening by the commune cadres.

The number of students that could be accepted by the universities or colleges was very small compared to the many millions of youngsters who had joined the Red Guards and then the "Up to the Mountains, Down to the Countryside" movement, and lost their education for seven years. The competition was keen beyond imagination. Pan was determined to seize this opportunity. He studied day and night. He even did not go to the hangar to work. The factory Chief and secretary seemed to be supporting him. Yeh was happy to see the young man studying hard and progressing day by day.

In early August of 1973, Pan received the acceptance letter. He was admitted to enroll in the Engineering College of Central China, at Wuhan, in September. He was overwhelmingly exulted. The whole factory was excited for him too, as he was the only soul being accepted out of the whole commune of more than five hundred young adults. However, rumors spread that Pan's admission was obtained through the "back door." Gossip held that his father was a so-called "high cadre (高幹)," a high-ranking official of the Communist Party.

Pan was the only welder in the factory. He recommended Yeh to take his place when he left for school, as he knew Yeh understood the fundamentals of electricity, and the arc welding required the knowledge of electricity. Pan taught Yeh some of the tricks in return.

A few weeks later, Yeh received a letter from Pan to tell his roommates how he was happy with life in his school. He especially mentioned the good meals in school. They could have meat or fish for every lunch and dinner. The school was certainly treating the students well; the meat ration in the commune was only half a pound a month. Workers in the factory could only expect to taste meat once a week.

The first of January is a worldwide holiday. That day in 1974 happened to be on Tuesday. It was a long weekend. Yeh and his roommates got permission from the factory Chief to go to Wuhan to visit Pan, as he had invited them to. Pan met them at the gate of the school. He was much better-looking in the new student uniform than in the patched and hardly cleaned, grayish-blue Mao suit. He was proud to show his old roommates their spacious dormitory, especially the indoor plumbing.

The buildings in the school must have been constructed long before the revolution and had not been kept well for many years, as there were chips showing everywhere. Facing the gate, an oversized portrait of Mao hung on the wall. Two red boards of equal height attached on each side had inscribed the slogan, "Down with the Counterrevolutionary Scholars! Long Live Chairman Mao's Educational Line!" It showed that the Cultural Revolution still remained strong in the school. There were many large posters of slogans hung conspicuously. To Yeh's surprise, some of them seemed to be posted completely contradictory to the place for higher education, such as, "We would rather have illiterate working people, not educated spiritual aristocrats." It was obvious that the country needed to learn foreign technology to improve its economy. Yet the poster advocated, "Learning from foreigners is just sniffing their farts and calling them a good smell." Some of the slogans criticized Confucius; even Pan frequently recited Mao's thoughts on education, such as, "Political indoctrination is more important than learning technology."

At a used bookstore near the school, Yeh was also surprised to see many old English magazines piled up at a corner. How could those magazines survive through the Red Guard catastrophe? They had burned all the reactionary books. They probably did not have the intelligence to distinguish whether those English magazines were antirevolutionary or not. Yeh bought quite a few of them.

Back at the plant, arc welding was mostly used to repair damaged tools. The welder did not have to stand by a machine or work bench eight hours a day. He could rest in the hangar and wait for a job to come. Yeh found it was a good time to read the English magazines. He had not touched any English publications for more than ten years. It was hard to read, as so many words were not comprehensible. Even though some words looked familiar, he could not grasp their exact meaning in that sentence. There was no dictionary available. He read it very slowly and had to read the same article many times to understand the real theme of it.

One day the Party secretary came to ask him:

"What you reading?"

"An English magazine."

"You understand English?"

"Not much. I have not read any English books for more than ten years. I have almost forgotten all of it. Hopefully, I can refresh my English by reading these magazines."

"Why do you want to learn English?"

"It seems to me the government is encouraging people to learn English now. You have probably heard the radio station teaching English every morning."

Yeh tried to defend himself. The radio station started to teach English alphabets and simple conversation since last summer.

"But beware of the Western influence. I don't want to see you being poisoned by those corrupted American lifestyles and capitalist thinking."

"Thank you for your advice!"

The other workers in the factory had a different point of view. "*Lao Yeh*, how wonderful you can read English! You will earn big money after you are released from the commune," Sun once said in front of many colleagues. The others seemed to respect him more.

The growing interactions of trade with other countries, the frequent dispatching of teams to participate in international athletic competitions or conferences, and receiving the increasing number of expatriate Chinese visiting the homeland all required English-speaking interpreters. But there were scarcely enough English-speaking natives available for this job.

All the schools in Communist China encouraged students to study Russian in order to learn from the big brother of Communism after 1949. To study English was suspected to have the intention of learning capitalism. Then the persecution of intellectuals following the "Let a hundred flowers bloom" movement and the Cultural Revolution eliminated most of the people who had a formal English education before. Even the few who survived through all these troubled years were well over fifty. They were regarded as a generation too old to participate in the political training for interpreters in this country. Even so, another restriction permitted only those politically correct people to contact foreigners.

The foreign diplomatic and business organizations had to recruit Chinese-speaking citizens, mostly Chinese descendents, from their own countries to do this job. Many of them came from the British colony of Hong Kong. Some of them came from America. They should definitely have been paid at least the same amount as they would earn in their own countries, in spite of the huge difference of average income between Communist China and their own countries. For the local government-recruited interpreters, they had to be paid well in order not to lose face in front of the foreigners. There soon came a class of well-dressed Chinese-looking people appearing in the big cities. They enjoyed meals and entertainment in the fancy hotels or nightclubs specially set aside for foreigners. They had a way to access high-quality foreign goods. They always had plenty of pocket money to spend. They were admired and envied. A public consensus soon evolved that learning English was a good way to get rich.

To Yeh, reading the English magazine was pure enjoyment. It often provided him some sense of human life, not like the Chinese media full of revolutionary clichés. Besides the propaganda and indoctrination, denunciation and accusation appeared in the rest of the Chinese publications. Any sentimental or melancholy writings were criticized as bourgeois vice. Yeh did not miss any opportunity to go to Wuhan to find some other English literature, even though each time he had to find an excuse to request a travel permit from Chief Zheng.

The Chinese New Year of 1975 drew near. Some workers in the factory were planning to travel a long way to reunite with their families. Yeh was called to the Party secretary's office. A cadre named Xu from the Air Force Political Department of PLA was there too. Xu told Yeh:

"*Lao* Yeh, I have good news for you. Our superior has decided to transfer you to a factory in Wuhan."

"Do you mean that I can leave the commune now? I have completed the reeducation?"

"You are perfectly right. You can report to my office after the New Year vacation. I will take you there."

It was really good news to Yeh. The Party secretary of the Red Army Production Brigade told him that he would be reeducated in the farm tool factory for another three years when he was transferred from Huang's village. He had never expected this kind of news, as he had only been in the factory for a few months over two years.

Cadre Xu told Yeh how to find his office in Wuhan and left. The whole factory soon heard the news; many workers came to congratulate him. They congratulated him not for being released from the commune; they congratulated him for having a chance to move to a big city.

After the Communist Party took over mainland China, Mao said, "People are power." He encouraged people to reproduce. Many directives were authorized to benefit the families with high birth rates. The population, in spite of the fact that many millions of people died in man-made famine, doubled in twenty years. The population pressure, especially in the big cities, had reached its limit. The "Up to the Mountains, Down to the Countryside" movement did help to reduce the pressure in the big cities. Then a totally different, almost completely opposite policy was adapted that persuaded people to practice birth control with contraceptives, and promoted strictly controlled the migration of people from rural to urban areas. Everybody knew that life in the big cities was much better than life in the countryside. Yet all of the people that had been moved from cities to the countryside during the late 1960s, following the honest, legal procedure, and would never be able to move back to their original urban residence.

Chapter Six: Unexpected Promotion

The so-called factory was a large-sized motor vehicle service station located in Hanyang, a city of Wuhan. Wuhan is the metropolitan area including three closely connected cities where the Han River merges with the Yangtze River, with Hankou on the north of both rivers, Wuchang on the southeast of Yangtze River, and Hanyang on the west of both rivers. Hankou is the commercial center of the whole region. Wuchang, the capital of Hubie Province, is the place where the revolution led by the KMT in 1911 began, which toppled the Qing Dynasty and established the Republic of China. It was the cultural and military center of that area. Hanyang was mostly residential with some light industries. The population in Wuhan exceeded three million. As there was a bridge over the Han River connecting Hankou and Hanyang, and a bridge over the Yangtze River connecting Hanyang and Wuchang, Hanyang became the midtown between these two big cities.

When Yeh arrived in the service station in January 1975, it had a staff of more than one hundred. All the vehicles being serviced there were either imported from Russia or indigenously manufactured. Yeh was assigned to work in the body shop to take over the arc-welding job. The lead man asked him to help others in doing some odd jobs such as sanding and polishing whenever there was no job requiring welding.

Yeh found the living environment in the station better than that in the commune. Happily, the Party secretary of the station did not closely monitor and indoctrinate the workers. There was no morning ritual of worshipping Mao. There was only an evening meeting once a week, and the meeting did not include mandatory self-criticism.

The employees received a salary and all kinds of food tickets and cloth tickets instead of receiving rations, as in the commune. People could buy anything available with their own money along with tickets. People could also trade unused tickets for money or vise versa in the black market. Here, people could manage their official share of supply to fit their own needs. For those goods without ticket requirement attached, the buyer had to show the supplier the evidence (work ID card) proving that he was a legal resident of Wuhan.

Yeh realized that the workers in the factory did not need a permit to leave the service station after the working hours, and all the people living in the city seemed to have bicycles. He decided to buy a bicycle for moving around this big city. He was anxious to visit the used bookstores to find some English literature to read, especially a good English dictionary. However, his lead man told him that he would be paid thirty-five RMB a month, which was barely enough for paying daily living expenses. He finally bought a used bicycle with almost all his savings.

The workers in the bachelor quarters of the service station were mostly young adults in their late twenties. They did not have much interest in getting to know a new man over forty, like Yeh. They had their way to enjoy life after working hours. Yeh went with his roommates to see Hankou on one Saturday afternoon, but found no common interest to go out together often.

Two weeks later Cadre Xu came to see him again.

"How do you like the job here, *Lao* Yeh?"

"I think it's okay. I think everybody has to work to earn a living."

"*Lao* Kuo told me to take care of you. He is now a division director of the PLAAF headquarters."

Yeh suddenly remembered Xu was one of the three cadres accompanied Kuo to meet him at the bus station near the Red Flag Commune two years ago. Xu must have known Yeh's background.

"I am very glad to hear that Kuo had another promotion. I think you know I have parents living in Taiwan. It has been twelve years since I left them. I miss them very much. Kuo promised me that I would be released to Taiwan when the time is right. Have you ever heard any news about this from him?"

Yeh dared not mention that he was a captured Republic of China U-2 pilot from Taiwan and that General Liu Yalou, the commander of the People's Liberation Army Air Force, had promised him, "If you want to go back to Taiwan to unite with your family, we can let you go after the investigation is completed." He had strictly followed Kuo's order not to mention any of this to anybody after being transferred from Beijing to the commune.

"I know you were once a KMT pilot. Director Kuo told me you would be released someday. I think you have to be patient. In the meantime, if you have any problem, you can contact me at my office."

Cadre Xu's office was in Wuchang. He left his telephone number for Yeh. From that time on, Xu came to see Yeh almost every month.

One time when Xu came to see him, Yeh said to Xu, "I heard that some people are working to get a passport to go abroad to visit their relatives. Others are applying to study in foreign countries. I know I was guilty for doing something against the People's Republic of China, but after eight years of incarceration and more than three years of reeducation, I should be permitted to go to Taiwan to visit my parents like an ordinary citizen. Would you please help me in this matter?"

"*Lao* Yeh, you have to be patient. To tell you the truth, Director Kuo mentioned your problem not long ago and said he would like to help you, but the political climate is not clear now. We have to be very careful."

The political climate was indeed under a dark cloud expecting a huge tornado to arrive soon in the latter part of 1975. Rumors circulated around that Premier Zhou Enlai was very sick that his prostate cancer had reached the terminal stage. Chairman Mao's health was even worse. He was so weak that no one could understand his blurry words spoken with a heavy Hunan accent. Only his wife Jiang Qing claimed she could understand him. Jiang Qing became Chairman Mao's spokeswoman. No one dared to question her about what Mao really meant. In spite of her corrupt life, Jiang Qing was supported by three cronies to form the so-called "Gang of Four" (四人幫). The Gang of Four led the revolutionary zealots pressing on the Cultural Revolution against modernization, which was led by Deng Xiaoping and his pragmatic faction in the Communist Party. Although most people looked forward to a better life and hated the struggle between them, no one could predict what would happen in the future.

Another politically turbulent year in Communist China was 1976. Premier Zhou died in January. Zhou was regarded as the only reasonable man among the Communist leaders. His statesmanship did mitigate the severity of destruction during the Red Guard era. He led the country out of its self-imposed isolation away from the free world. Without his intercession, people worried that the modernization efforts might not be able to survive.

Yeh noticed that the revolutionary radicals in the service station became more active in criticizing others for lack of political progress in the evening meetings. The Big Character Posters reappeared on the walls of busy streets to denounce those recently rehabilitated ranking officials who were regarded as staging a capitalist-revisionist comeback. People had lost their enthusiasm for supporting another revolutionary movement, and they complained privately about the possibility of losing the improvements in life since Deng had been reinstalled to his old post.

The fifth of April 1976 was the date of the Spring Festival (清明節) in China. The festival is the traditional time for people to visit their family graves and memorialize their ancestors. As the festival approached, some people in Beijing bravely sent wreaths of white flowers along with couplets on white scrolls to the revolutionary martyrs in Tiananmen Square in memory of Premier Zhou. This excited the masses around Beijing. Wreathes and banners with memorial poems on them kept coming until the huge square was full. Students and intellectuals wearing black armbands lined up on the long Changan Street to pay tribute to the late premier. Many memorial poems clearly protested against the radicals. Mourning for Zhou soon turned into a mammoth demonstration. The people's voice needed to be heard by those high-ranking cadres living in Zhungnanhai, the new Forbidden City of Communist China.

In the night of the Spring Festival, armed police joined radicals to remove wreathes and banners, and to drive the demonstrators out of Tiananmen Square, amid street clashes and arrests. Vice Premier Deng was accused as the man behind the demonstration and banished from his post again. Class struggles intensified in the rest of the country. Yet the pragmatic factions did not give up easily this time.

Three months later in July, a powerful earthquake shook Tangshan, the biggest coal-mining city in China, located ninety miles east of Beijing. It made the whole city into ruins, killed more than a quarter-million people, and scared the people in that region, including Beijing, into remaining out of their houses for many days until the aftershocks subsided. Then a gigantic meteor fell in Jilin Province northeast of Tangshan. All these unusual occurrences diverted people's attention from the class struggle. Some regarded these events bad omens, which preceded the fall of a dynasty, as that had happened many times in the four thousand years of Chinese history.

At three o'clock in the afternoon on September 9, the loudspeakers around the service station surprisingly asked workers to stop working and be ready to listen to important news. A few minutes later, the Party secretary of the service station broadcast in a sad voice that Mao had passed away. Twenty-six days later, Jiang Qing and her Gang of Four were arrested. People were excited and went out into the streets to celebrate. Deng resumed the post of vice premier. The pragmatic faction was gradually assuming power.

People were mostly very happy, yet Hua Guofeng, who succeeded Mao as the chairman of the Communist Party, ordered the people to carry out "all Chairman Mao's policies" and to obey "all Chairman Mao's directives." Hua was comparatively junior in the hierarchy of the Communist Party and almost unknown to the public. He had no massive, hard core to support him. Rumors circulated that he was an illegitimate son of Chairman Mao. Nevertheless, the radicals still sought to hold on to their special privileges acquired during the Cultural Revolution, as no one dared to say anything wrong about Mao's teachings. Fortunately, Yeh did not belong to either the radicals or the pragmatic faction. He was spared to read his favorite English literatures.

Later, in the spring of 1977, Cadre Xu came and said to Yeh:
"I was told that you are studying English."
"Yes, I just read English magazines to pass the time."
"Can you translate English into Chinese?"
"Depends on what kind of English."

Xu showed him a few pages of English print. It must have been a copy of an article published in some American magazine. As so many typographical errors appeared, the typist must not have had a good understanding of English. The article reported on the competition to develop a lightweight fighter in the United States. After three years' hard work, General Dynamics was finally selected over Northrop Aircraft Company to be the winner of the prototype program. It would continue with full-scale engineering development in January 1975. The fighter was named the F-16. It was the first report of an aircraft Yeh had ever seen since he landed in the mainland. To a military jet pilot, it was certainly an interesting subject that he wanted to learn more about.

"I would like to try. How soon do you need it?"
"I'm not in a hurry. You can keep it as long as you need for translation."

The fastest airplane Yeh had ever flown was an RF-101, which could reach 1.2 Mach, i.e., 1.2 times the speed of sound. He was fascinated that an F-16 could fly twice the speed of sound. It could withstand a G-force of nine (nine times the earth's gravitational force), more than the 7.33 Gs of other jet fighters. That meant the F-16 had more maneuverability in combat. The control stick was now installed on the right console instead of mounted on the floor between the pilot's legs, as in all conventional aircraft. All the combat-related switches were mounted on the handle of either the control stick or the throttle, so that pilot did not have to stretch out his arms to reach any switch in the cockpit while in combat. The bubble-type canopy had no frame to block the pilot's view. Many of the new designs—a fly-by-wire control system, a heads-up display, etc.—were beyond his comprehension. It took quite a while for him to figure out how to translate them, no matter whether the translation was correct or not.

Two weeks later, Yeh delivered the translation in Chinese to Cadre Xu's office. Xu himself could not read English. He just said, "Very good. Thank you."

The next time Cadre Xu came to see Yeh, Xu brought an American Air Force dictionary with him and asked Yeh to translate it as well.

"*Lao* Xu, are you kidding? You must have overestimated my ability. This is a dictionary. This is a two hundred-some-page dictionary. You think I can translate a dictionary?"

"*Lao* Yeh, don't be so modest. The responsible section of our division thought you had done a very good job on the translation of the F-16 article. They said you were probably the only one in our Air Force to understand the American Air Force terminology."

"It is so big a job! How can I do that in this automobile service station? I have to work in the daytime. I don't even have a personal desk. I can hardly have any quiet time for myself in my room."

"Don't worry about that. These can all be arranged." Xu said.

The next week, Yeh was assigned to the maintenance section to assist a technician in charge of the electrical systems of the facility. He was also told to move to a better room, equipped with two beds, two desks with chairs, and a closet, which Yeh shared with another lead man. His salary also was raised to fifty-six RMB. The first thought he had was he would be able to buy better meals to entertain Xu from that time on, as "connections" in China were so important. Even going through the "back door," one needed a connection. Yet Xu was the only connection Yeh knew who might reach the ranking officials in the Communist Party who controlled his fate.

There was not much routine electrical maintenance work. Occasionally the technician led Yeh to answer a call to correct a short or replace a fuse. Less frequently he had to follow his leader to climb up to the ceiling or electric pool to rearrange the power lines. When there was no call Yeh could stay in his room to work on the translation and enjoy reading other English literature.

The spring rainy season ended slowly in 1978. People were making pyramid-shaped pudding (粽子) by wrapping the rice with bamboo leaves. It was the time to prepare for the annual Dragon Boat Festival (端午節). Yeh's translation work had reached the stage of typesetting and final proofreading; Cadre Xu came to tell Yeh more good news:

"*Lao* Yeh, I would like to congratulate you this time. Our Party has decided to appoint you as an English instructor in the Engineering College of Central China at Wuchang."

"*Lao* Xu, you have confused me. Tell me what happened!"

Yeh really was confused. He had never dreamed of teaching English in a college. How could the college employ an instructor with his political background? He had not even heard that there would be an opening for English instructors.

"*Lao* Yeh, times have changed, you know. Deng Xiaoping instructed the Party to ask 'professionals' to solve problems. He said, 'Black cat or white cat, a mouse-catcher is a good cat.' The colleges are now selecting students through open entrance examination without considering whether the applicant is from a 'black, red, or white' family. The schools are also recruiting capable teachers and asking various organizations to recommend them. Our division recommended you. I just heard that you have been accepted."

"What should I do then?"

"Wait to receive an official notice. You know the instructor can earn more or less 100 RMB a month. It is almost twice as much as your salary now. I think we should have a big celebration."

A lavish banquet was arranged that evening. Besides Xu, Yeh's supervisor, the Party secretary and the Chief of the service station, and several other colleagues were also invited. Without any hesitation, Yeh spent a major portion of his savings to pay all the expenses.

Two weeks later, the expected official notice still did not show up. Yeh called Xu:

"*Lao* Xu, are you pulling my leg? I have not seen any official notice so far."

"It should not be that way. I know definitely that the Provincial Revolutionary Committee had approved your transfer. It must be some stubborn radicals trying to stall the process or waiting for graft. Don't worry. I will take care of it."

The official paper finally arrived. Yeh rode his bicycle across the bridge between Hanyang and Wuchang to the college. The school had not changed much since Yeh visited three and half years ago, when Pan proudly showed him and his roommates in the commune tool factory the good accommodations. The only difference was all the revolutionary slogans had disappeared. The huge portraits of Mao still occupied the most conspicuous position on the façade and in the courtyards.

He reported to the department head, Jiang. He seemed not very enthusiastic to have another faculty member to share the teaching load. After a few words of greeting, Jiang introduced himself briefly. He had graduated from Wuhan University when the school had retreated to Sichuan Province during the war against the Japanese. His underground activity in school won him a membership of the Communist Party in the early 1950s. He had never had any trouble in any political movement, as he always strictly followed the Party line no matter what direction the political wind blew.

Then Jiang asked Yeh politely many questions about his background. To Jiang it is very unusual to transfer a worker in the automobile service station to fill out a position of English instructor in college. Yeh must have a connection with some high-ranking cadre in Party Central (黨中央). He also doubted Yeh had the capability to teach English. As Yeh did not have any satisfactory answers to provide, he finally led Yeh to the faculty quarters and told Yeh a room in a bungalow would be evacuated for him in a week.

Yeh traveled back and forth several times to move his belongings to the school by bicycle. The room was big enough for a bed, a desk with chair, a closet, and a rack for a washbasin. The tiled floor was much easier to clean than the mud floor in those rooms he had lived in the past six years, despite the fact that many of the tiles were broken. The back door of this room led to a kitchen and a latrine shared by all six families living in that bungalow. He noticed his neighbors had to live in the same size of rooms with their whole families. He felt fortunate. He remembered his roommate in the commune village, Qin, told him after his attempted suicide, "God has a plan for everybody." This might be the plan God had for him. He should try his best to glorify it.

Yeh met two other English associate professors and three other instructors in the faculty office. The instructors were all so called "worker-farmer-soldier students" graduated from different universities recently. The associate professors were both rehabilitated from rural communes three years ago. Their hardships in and out of prison camps and communes had consumed their health and spirit. Teaching was only a job to earn a living.

At the Engineering College of Central China, English was the only foreign language taught in the school, and it was only taught in the first year of undergraduate education. The students were expected to acquire the capability to read English technical publications and write some simple essays in English. Jiang told Yeh to select teaching materials from English translations of Chairman Mao's writings, Party documents, and periodicals. Yeh spent much time going through these publications trying to find appropriate materials for texts. He was quite disappointed as only a few met his own criteria. First, those English publications were mostly translations of Chinese documents. There was no one-to-one correspondence between Chinese and English. Without reference of the original Chinese documents, it was very difficult to explain them in Chinese correctly to the students. He also had to be very careful about this, for all the students were brought up under the Communist regime. Second, the contents of those documents were either indoctrination or propaganda, which he hated from the bottom of his heart. How could he translate them open-mindedly to the students?

As there was not much time left before the new semester started in September, he decided to increase the proportion of English grammar in the curriculum as much as he could, because that would not involve "unacceptable" politics.

Preparing the lecture notes and correcting students' homework, in addition to the twelve hours of classroom teaching every week, made Yeh very busy. As there was no typewriter available that could type both English and Chinese together, so he spent much time writing the lecture notes on stencil and then making copies to hand out in class. Teaching also provided Yeh a good opportunity to learn. He had to answer many of the questions correctly about English that the students asked, which he generally had ignored before. Yeh also spent a lot of time searching for the answers in the library. He was literally growing with the students.

Besides the busy life of teaching, Yeh realized that without much political struggle Chinese society became more relaxed. The economy had improved slightly. One piece of the headline news, which people liked to talk about, was the official visit of Deng Xiaoping to the United States in January 1979, right after the United States formally established diplomatic relations with PRC and severed the diplomatic relations with ROC in Taiwan. Deng was received as the head of a state, even though he was the vice chairman of the Chinese Communist Party.

The United States did not object to the claim that Taiwan was a part of China as PRC. Official documents gradually revealed that the PRC regarded the government in Taiwan as a rebel provincial government. They treated the people in Taiwan as a special kind of citizen (台胞) in between the foreigners and the ordinary citizens, in order to allure investment. They recognized that the economy in Taiwan was much more advanced than the PRC and was praised worldwide as one of the four economic dragons, along with South Korea, Hong Kong, and Singapore in the developing countries. Yeh's colleagues who knew he was a KMT officer gradually became less serious about "drawing a distinct line against the class enemy" in their daily contacts with him.

His busy life made the time pass quickly. The first semester ended just a few days before the Chinese New Year of 1979. After he completed grading the students' final examination, he felt like he had passed the qualification test of an instructor in the college.

As the general comments about him by the students were favorable, many parents came to ask him to teach their children English. Under the new strict regulation of one child per family, parents cared very much about their only child. They all had the pathetic experience of being deprived of education in the name of the Cultural Revolution. They did not want to see their only child going through the same situation, and were willing to spend money—as much as they could—to provide their child the best education. Yeh always declined them politely because he did not have enough spare time, until Ouyang came to ask him to be the English tutor of her son. She could not be easily denied.

Ouyang was a very powerful woman. She was the Party secretary at the engineering college. Her husband was a member of the Provincial Revolution Committee. Yeh had better not refuse her. Her son, Zhang Guanghua, was a first-year high school student. If he could provide a satisfactory service, Yeh would have an influential ally. He went to Ouyang's home to teach Guanghua two evenings a week voluntarily.

Wuhan is the famous "hot pot" of central China in the summer. The teachers were fortunate to have summer recess about two months long. Yeh could take a long nap in the afternoon under the breeze provided by an electric fan. He could stay late in the night to enjoy reading or other amusements when the temperature was lower.

One day in August, Yin, an instructor in the physics department, invited Yeh to participate in a banquet. A banquet was arranged by Yin to thank those who had helped him in obtaining the scholarship of a graduate school in the United States. He came to see Yeh in the spring to solicit help in filling out the application forms and correct errors in the recommendation letters he had drafted for the undersigned. He was ready to go abroad next week.

At the banquet the guests congratulated Yin as if he was ready to ascend to paradise in heaven. Everybody thought that life in the United States was what was shown in the American movies. Yin also told the guests how difficult it was to apply for a passport and the long line waiting in applying for a visa at the American consulate.

It seemed to Yeh the government had relaxed the control of going abroad, since Yin was not a privileged child of high-ranking cadres. He bought two cartons of imported cigarettes and two bottles of brandy through a friend of Pan. Pan had graduated from the college and had been assigned to work for a power factory in Guangdong Province two years earlier. Yeh brought these gifts to Cadre Xu.

"*Lao* Yeh. You are so nice to me. What can I do for you?"

"A few days ago, I was invited to participate in a farewell party. A friend of mine was leaving for the United States. He told us how he applied for a passport and visa. I think the government has changed the policy on traveling out of the country. I think there may be a chance for me to go back to Taiwan. Would you please contact Kuo to see if he can consider my case again?"

"I know you are anxious to go to see your parents. But your case is different. Remember, three years ago we talked about the same subject and I said the political climate is not clear. I did not tell you the whole picture."

Yeh remembered Xu did say that. He thought the political climate pointed to the struggle between the radicals and the pragmatics. Xu continued:

"To tell you the truth, by the same time you were transferred from the commune to the automobile factory, more than three hundred arrested KMT officers were also released from various communes and prisons by the order of Vice Premier Deng. Ten generals among them requested to go to Taiwan because their families had moved there before they were captured in the mainland. They applied for entrance permits to Taiwan after arriving in Hong Kong, through the KMT consulate there. They waited and waited. No response was ever received."

Yeh thought Xu must have been trying to discourage him. Yet Xu continued:

"You know what? Some months later, from our intelligence source we finally understood the reason was that Chiang Kaishek had said, 'It is a motto of the People's Revolution Army (國民革命軍, the army that overthrew the Qing Dynasty and wiped out the warlords to establish the central government of China before World War II) that **if you could not succeed, sacrifice yourself** (不成功,便成仁). No prisoner of war is welcome to come back.' No one in Taiwan could appeal their cases because Chiang was old and very sick, at the terminal stage of life. One of the generals was so disappointed he committed suicide in his hotel room in Hong Kong."

Yeh did not respond, as he could not tell whether this was a true story. Even if this was a true story, the situation was different now, as Chiang Kaishek had died several years ago. The government policy in Taiwan might have changed. He did not want to let Xu know any of his doubts. Xu continued:

"By the way, I met Ouyang at a meeting the other day. She commended you highly. You should have a bright future in the college."

Soon the new semester started. Yeh resumed his busy teaching life. Occasionally he noticed the newspaper posted a new kind of article that reported the authorization by the government to reverse the sentences of victims (平反) wrongly accused during the Cultural Revolution and various other political campaigns. Many high-ranking officials were reinstalled in their old positions and paid their withheld salary. One of the cases in February 1980 was inconceivable to Yeh. That was the announcement of removing all the charges and punishments against President Liu Shaoqi. But everybody knew that Liu died in prison many years ago, for Mao had refused to provide medical care. Yeh talked to a colleague:

"Everybody knows Premier Liu died in prison many years ago. This announcement has no practical meaning at all."

"*Lao* Yeh, you do not know it is very important in China. Chairman Mao said: 'Dragon breeds dragon, phoenix breeds phoenix, the son of rat can only dig holes.' If his case were not clarified, all his descendents, from his children down, would be listed as from a family of a renegade (叛徒), a traitor (內奸), and a scab (工賊). They would be discriminated against for generations to come."

Many renowned scholars and scientists prosecuted during various movements were also restored to good standing, one after another. One of them was a professor in Yeh's school. Dr. Qien Weichang (錢偉長) was his name. He was a Ph.D. from MIT and a well-recognized scholar for his contributions to fluid mechanics. He returned to China to participate in building a new China in the early 1950s. He was later accused as a rightist and went through all kinds of reeducation until being rehabilitated a few years ago.

The announcement that removed all of Dr. Qien's false accusations from his record did lift his spirits. He began to devote his time, besides teaching, to continuing his research in his special field. He planned to publish a periodical, *Chinese Journal of Fluid*

Mechanics, to provide an opportunity for scholars in China to present their research results and to learn what others were doing in research. He also planned to publish an English version of this journal in order to have communication with scholars in other countries. He selected two associate professors in his department to be the editors of the English version of the journal.

As the manuscripts went through reviewing and editing, the final copy of the publication was submitted to Qien for approval. He was disappointed by the English writing, which in no way could be presented to the scholars in the English-speaking countries. He tried to seek help by distributing several copies of a manuscript to the faculties of the English department, asking them to correct the mistakes.

When all the copies were returned to Dr. Qien's office, it was probably because only Yeh was taking this job so conscientiously; he decided Yeh was the right man for the position of Chief editor. He would like to promote Yeh to be an associate professor to avoid the conflict of two associate professors supervised by an English instructor in the editors' office. It was a very unusual recommendation. Both the English department head and the college president objected to the promotion, as Yeh had only worked as instructor for just three years. But the Party secretary, Ouyang, had a different opinion. She spoke for Yeh. She was a powerful woman in the college. No one cared to argue with this woman. In the summer of 1981, Yeh was authorized yet another unexpected promotion.

Chapter Seven: Permission to Leave the Mainland

It was a tough challenge to Yeh to edit manuscripts for an English technical journal. He had to learn the meaning of fluid mechanic terminologies. Although he was not responsible for evaluating the technical contribution of the papers, he was supposed to iron out the glitches in every sentence to make it intelligible to English-speaking readers. All the authors were Chinese. The Chinese language does not differentiate among genders. There are no equivalent words to distinguish "he," "she," or "it" in Chinese conversation. There are no corresponding verbs following the first, second, or third person such as "am," "are," "is," "was," "were," "have been," "has been," or "had been." It is very difficult for them to memorize all the rules of English grammar on the tenses of a verb, the singular or the plural, the active or the passive voices, the subjective or objective cases, the articles and prepositions. Even Yeh was not sure himself in some cases of exceptional usages, which he had to find out by searching for examples in the library. Fortunately, he did not have to spend much time preparing lecture notes after teaching for six semesters on the same subjects. He also did not have to spend time tutoring Zhang Guanghua who had been accepted to continue his studies in English at a prestigious language school in Beijing after graduation from high school.

Along with his promotion, Yeh received better pay and was provided with better housing. That made his colleagues envious. He overheard someone say that he must have close ties with the Party secretary, Ouyang; otherwise, he would never be promoted this way. After all, he had not earned a degree in English literature from any university. No one mentioned his good work in English editing. On the other hand, Yeh noticed that people around him greeted him more politely and also kept some distance from him. He was glad about the change in his status. He was clearly aware how close the relationship he had with Ouyang was.

As Yeh understood, Ouyang was seven years his senior. When the Japanese surrendered to the Allies in 1954, she was a sophomore in a university in Guangdong Province and was persuaded by the Communist Front Organization to go to Yan'an, the headquarters of CCP at that time, to study in the Revolutionary University. She married Zhang, a member of the Hubei Provincial Revolutionary Committee, when he was a high-ranking officer in the People's Liberation Army later in the 1950s. Quanghua was her youngest son. She and her husband were both very active. For more than two years, Yeh had gone to her house generally twice a week to tutor Quanghua, though he had rarely seen her and her husband. A maid always came to open the door for him. Ouyang knew Yeh was born in Guangdong too. She occasionally spoke Guangdong dialect with Yeh, as most Guangdonese like to talk to each other in their own dialect, even among a group of people who do not understand it.

As the economy improved gradually in 1982, people were willing to spend more money to celebrate the Chinese New Year. All three of Ouyang's children came with their spouses and children to have a family reunion. Yeh was invited to join their New Year's Eve banquet. Quanghua was excited to tell Yeh about his happy experience in the language school, which had a department for foreign students matriculating to learn Chinese. The foreign students like to practice their Chinese and vice versa. They tried to get together whenever there was an opportunity. Quanghua was proud that his English pronunciation was better than that of his classmates, so he could easily mingle with the foreign students. He greatly enjoyed going to many of the nightclubs specially set aside for the foreigners. He remained grateful that Yeh had taught him the correct pronunciation.

An instructor in Wuhan University, a close friend of Ouyang's elder son, also was invited. He was ready to go to Canada to visit his older sister, whom he had never met because she had fled mainland China before he was born. Based on this weak link, he applied for a passport and was approved. Ouyang told them that the People's government had relaxed the restriction on traveling aboard. She said:

"Our Party would like to let people tell their relatives in foreign countries in person, including Hong Kong and Taiwan, of our progress under socialism. We also encourage their relatives to visit China and to invest in China."

After the banquet, Yeh found an opportunity to talk to Ouyang individually:

"Secretary Ouyang," he said, "you must know my situation. I miss my parents very much. No matter what I did, I am now an associate professor of this college. Could I apply for a passport to go to Taiwan?"

"*Lao* Yeh, I fully understand your situation. You know your case is different. I can help you visit Taiwan only if the PLAAF agrees."

"Could you ask the People's Liberation Army Air Force for me?"

"Well, I can try. It may take a quite a while, since yours is not an urgent case."

"I certainly can wait. I have been waiting for more than eighteen years already."

Three months later, Yeh was summoned to Ouyang's office.

"*Lao* Yeh, good news. The People's Liberation Army Air Force agrees to let you go. Now, you only have one problem."

Another problem! Ouyang had not mentioned this before. The Communists always had an excuse to harass people. It was not good news at all, Yeh thought.

"You are a college professor. You are valuable to the people. We can let you have a short visit to Taiwan, but we don't want to lose you. According to the regulations, you have to have someone guarantee that you will come back after the visit."

"Secretary, you know that I don't have any relatives living here. I don't have any good friends who would do that for me."

"Have you ever thought about getting married?"

"I am fifty years old. Who would want to marry an old man with a complex background?"

What Yeh really wanted to say the exact situation was, "In this 'draw a clear line of demarcation from class enemy' country, who would want to tangle with a possible candidate of a struggle, a target in the next political movement, and let her child be born a second-class citizen?"

"*Lao* Yeh, if you agree, the Party will find a good girl for you."

"Thanks be to the Party!"

"If that is the only way to obtain a passport to leave this country, I might as well follow the arrangement," Yeh thought.

He was told that his grandparents had been married by arrangement by their parents. They did not even see each other before the wedding. They lived happily thereafter and did not have any complaint about their marriage all their lives. On the other hand, he was also told that the Party arranged many marriages for the old revolutionary soldiers who were retired from the People's Liberation Army and assigned to various offices as Party functionaries. They were mostly uneducated and much older than their brides. The deep gap between husbands and wives on the different perspectives of matrimonial reunion created many troubled families. Some of the young girls even committed suicide to resist the arrangements. Yeh could not predict what would happen to his case. Maybe God has a special plan for him, as Qin said.

It was the end of another semester. Yeh was overseeing the students taking final examination, when a cadre came to tell him that Ouyang wanted to see him after the examination.

Ouyang told him that the Party had decided on the marriage of Yeh and a girl named Ding Xiaohung. She was thirty-one years old and the youngest daughter in a revolutionary "red" family. Yeh was supposed to meet her and her parents the following Saturday afternoon.

Yeh went to have a haircut and bought some candies and some popular cigarettes that Saturday morning. After lunch and a short nap, he wore a clean Mao suit and rode his bicycle, crossing the bridge over Yangtze River to Ding's residence in Hanyang. An old man with gray hair answered the gate.

"*Lao Bo*, I am Yeh Changsheng. May I see Mr. Ding?"

"I am Ding. You must be Professor Yeh. Secretary Ouyang told me about you. Please come in."

"Thank you, Ding *Lao Xiensheng* (老先生, old gentleman)."

It was a three-bedroom single house with a small yard enclosed within a brick wall. Yeh met Mrs. Ding and their daughter, Xiaohung, in the living room. She wore a grayish Mao suit with no makeup. Her two short braids draped over her shoulders. She looked younger than her age.

After the gifts were accepted, tea was served and a few greeting words exchanged, Ding began to ask many questions about Yeh's background and briefly told Yeh how he had followed Chairman Mao from being a son of a poor tenant farmer to becoming a member of the city revolutionary committee. He said:

"I was a poor peasant. I am still a peasant. I have no special skills. I don't understand much of the theory of Communism. But I loyally, passionately obey the Party's order."

His reverent attitude toward the only portrait on the whitewashed wall of the living room whenever he expressed his gratefulness to Chairman Mao made Yeh understand Ding was a committed Maoist. Ding then said:

"Xiaohung is our lovely daughter. The Party has decided that you and Xiaohung should be married. We have no objection to the

Party's directive. I think it is better to let you both talk about the marriage." Ding and his wife then left the room.

"Ding Xiaohung, you are a pleasant girl. I don't know whether you have known all my background. I am fifty years old. Do you think I am too old for you?" Yeh asked:

"My father said we should always obey the Party's decision."

"In that case, would you like to see the place where I live? If you agree, I will come tomorrow to take you to the college where I teach. We can get to know each other better in this way. I certainly would like to know you better."

The following Sunday was a bright day. Yeh realized that his life would have a drastic change in the near future. He was excited, although he could not foretell whether the change would be for the better or worse. He had almost forgotten how to treat a person of the opposite sex, especially since the person was supposed to live with him for the rest of his life.

Xiaohung was already waiting for him when Yeh arrived in her house. They rode on two bicycles, crossing the crowded bridge and coming to the school. There was no class in school on Sunday and the campus was comparably quiet. Yeh learned, while they were walking in the campus, that Xiaohung joined the Red Guards while she was in middle school and joined the "Up to the Mountains, Down to the Countryside" movement to learn from the peasants in the northwest rural area of Hubei Province. By her parents' connection, she was transferred back to the city and had worked in a textile mill since then.

"Did you experience any romance all these years?" Yeh asked

"What romance? That is a bourgeois poison weed."

"I mean, did you have any close boyfriend in all these years?"

"You know in the commune, although there were boys, we all lived like monks and nuns. No one was allowed to meet any boy alone. The textile mill has mostly female workers."

After a tour of his office and the classrooms, they went to his apartment. It was a one-bedroom apartment with private bathroom and kitchen. Yeh had not been in the mood to spend time on decorating the interior since he moved in a year ago. Besides a single bed and a closet in the bedroom, a desk and a chair in the living room, there was no other furniture.

"Xiaohung, how would you like to decorate this apartment? You girls know how to decorate the interior. You decide what kind of furniture you like. We can go out to look for them whenever you have time."

"I have decided to quit my job at the textile mill. We can go out whenever you have time."

They enjoyed a light lunch in the nearby restaurant, and talked like they had known each other for a long time. He did not propose and she did not wait for his proposal. Marriage was just a business deal. They talked about this business deal like starting a joint venture. They were willing to make this joint venture prosper, and there were many items to be discussed in detail.

The next day they got together again to continue working on their new nest. It was near dinnertime when he accompanied her back to her home. Xiaohung's mother came out to invite Yeh to have dinner with them.

"Ding *Lao Taitai*, thank you. I am afraid I have to go back to school to finish some paperwork tonight," Yeh answered

"Don't call me Ding *Lao Taitai*, Changsheng. You should call me Mother." She seemed happy to have Yeh as a son-in-law.

"Yes, Mother."

Three weeks after the end of the spring semester, a simple wedding ceremony for Yeh and Xiaohung was held in a conference room of the English department. Hard candies, cigarettes, and green tea were laid on the tables along the walls. Benches were filed in the middle for the guests. Ouyang and Jiang were the witnesses. Ouyang was very nice to lend her Red Flag automobile as the wedding limousine. Yeh went to Ding's house in the limousine to take the bride back to the ceremony site.

The bride and the bridegroom wearing new Mao suits with red corsages on their chests walked into the conference room to the guests' applause. After they bowed to Mao's portrait hanging on the wall behind the podium three times, Ouyang made a speech:

"… We are glad to have another new revolutionary family join the fighting force against capitalism and feudalism. I am sure the bride and the groom will devote their time and efforts to serving the people, and following Chairman Mao's teaching to establish a new 'proletariat dictatorship' socialism in China…."

The guests, including Yeh's in-laws, congratulated the newlywed at the end of the ceremony. Xiaohung's mother said to Yeh with tears in her eyes:

"This is really a match made by heaven. Changsheng, you know, I had introduced many good boys to Xiaohung. She did not like any of them. When Xiaohung's father told her about you, she agreed immediately. Xiaohung is my dearest baby. You will take good care of her, won't you?"

The wedding reception for relatives and close friends was held in the nearby restaurant. Ouyang and Jiang did not participate, for they had other engagements. Xiaohung's elder brother, a few of Yeh's colleagues, and Xu, the cadre from the PLLAF, forced him to drink more than he could tolerate, which made a lousy wedding night for Yeh. As he remembered the marriage with Betty, sex is an expression of love. The act of sex is trying to make your partner sensually happy. But that night, Yeh only recognized that they both had completed no more than a matrimonial ritual. He also realized Xiaohung was not a virgin, which made him feel less guilty, for he himself was not a virgin. He did not talk about this with Xiaohung.

There was not much to do for professors in the summer vacation. They selected a tour of the famous Three Gorges on the Yangtze River for their honeymoon, and caught a bus to go to Yichang and boarded a riverboat to cruise upstream to Chongqing. Sitting in a recliner on the top deck of a slow-moving riverboat watching the steep cliffs passing by was a wonderful interlude, the most pleasure

Yeh ever had since he landed on the mainland. All the dark clouds of political threat seemed far behind. He had been living alone for almost nineteen years. Infrequent conversation with Xiaohung made him aware that he was not alone anymore. Xiaohung enjoyed the scenery even more, as she had been accustomed to participating in all kinds of political movements, and had never had the luxury of such a leisure trip before.

It was late afternoon when they returned home by train. Yeh felt somewhat tired, but Xiaohung was still fairly energetic. She rode on bicycle to buy food and then cooked the dinner.

From the following day on, Yeh always went to his office in the morning, while the temperature was still mild, to catch up the editing work he had left behind during the two weeks' honeymoon. He was happy that Xiaohung always had lunch ready when he arrived home. The food tasted much better than the food in the school dining hall, where he had had meals every day for the past four years. Sometimes in the late afternoon they bicycled to tour some scenic spots around Wuhan. Yeh liked to go up to the hilltop of Yellow Crane Tower, where he could have a clear view of the Yangtze River and the bridge over it in the cool breeze. Yeh also liked to enjoy evenings in the teahouse close to the river, watching the lighted riverboats moving around. Although Yeh had lived in Wuhan so many years, he had never been in the mood to enjoy these places all by himself.

One morning in August, Yeh was awakened by a strange noise in the bathroom. It sounded like Xiaohung was vomiting. He got up immediately to find out what had happened to her. She looked pale with tears in her eyes. She was definitely ill. Yeh insisted on taking her to see a doctor.

After about twenty minutes' consultation, the doctor came out his office with Xiaohung and said:

"Congratulations, Professor Yeh. Your 'lover' (爱人) is pregnant."

Ever since the Communists seized power, they had advocated the equality of men and women. There should not be any husband or wife in a family. They should call "lover." He heard Xiaohung mention him as "my lover" to other persons several times. But from a person whom he had never known before, in the middle of the waiting room with many patients around, the calling of "your lover is pregnant" inevitably caused Yeh some embarrassment.

"Thank you, Doctor. I am sorry that I was so ignorant."

"Don't feel bad. Many couples came to me, just like you, without knowing that the female comrade has been pregnant for more than two months. Their parents did not educate them about how a baby is conceived. The old generation still regards sex as too taboo to tell their children about."

"What the doctor has said! Xiaohung has been pregnant for more than two months? We have only been married a few days more than a month. Did the doctor make a wrong diagnosis? Anyway, it is not the place or the time to find out what is wrong in the middle of a crowd." Yeh talked to himself without making a sound, and then he said.

"Doctor what should we do now?"

"You have nothing to worry about. The morning sickness usually comes when the stomach is empty."

That morning in his office Yeh could not concentrate on reviewing the manuscripts. He felt like being cheated.

"No wonder Xiaohung's mother had said, 'I introduced many good boys to Xiaohung. She did not like any of them. When Xiaohung's father told her about you. She agreed immediately.' Xiaohung must have found herself pregnant before she agreed to marry me. No matter how the Communists claimed liberation, there still was no place for an unwed mother and her illegitimate child in this chastity-ridden society. Even her parents would be disgraced by this scandal. I have heard many stories in the past years about a girl who bled to death after seeking an abortion from a backstreet midwife to get rid of the fetus from casual sex, and about a boy beating his mother to death and then committing suicide for not being able to stand being called 'bastard' and being discriminated against every way.… Xiaohung must have been desperate to find a foolish guy to be her husband to cover up her immoral behavior. I just happened to be that foolish guy," Yeh thought.

"Could the doctor make a wrong diagnosis? Xiaohung looked so innocent. She did not look like a woman of easy virtue. I should not hastily jump to a conclusion, especially at this moment. The application for my passport has been submitted. I should not raise any issue to jeopardize the process of getting the permit to go to Taiwan, which I have been looking forward to for so many years. Besides, I have married the present Xiaohung, not the past Xiaohung," Yeh thought.

At lunch Xiaohung asked:
"Changsheng, you look like something is bothering you."
"Xiaohung, who is the father of the baby?"
Xiaohung caught her breath in surprise for a little while, and then said:

"Changsheng, I thought I could start a new life by marrying you. Obviously heaven chose not to forgive me for what I have done before. I am very sorry for not telling you everything before the wedding.

"About a year ago, my factory appointed a new section Chief. After a few weeks of familiarization, he decided to select a worker to help him manage some paperwork in his office. I was happy to be selected, as I did not have to stand by the machine all day long anymore, and to get a raise also.

"Six months later, I asked him why he did not go back to his home in Shanghai as most people do when the factory closed for the New Year holidays. I knew he had his wife and a child there. He said he did not get along with his wife.

"Before the Chinese New Year I was asked to work overtime to help him close all accounts and prepare the annual report. For about ten days, we stayed in the office until late at night. He always bought dinner for me. When the report was done, we went to a popular restaurant in Hangkuo to cerebrate the good work we had completed. He told me he had asked his wife for a divorce and would like to show me the letters between him and his wife at his apartment.

"He was gentle to me. He said I was his dream girl. You know, I had no experience with being so close to a man. My parents watched me very closely all these years. I thought I was in love. He said he knew how to protect me from becoming pregnant. But I was always worried very much afterward. I dare not tell my mother about this.

"Five months passed; his wife still did not agree to divorce. I felt like I had been exploited. I thought I had to stop this unhealthy relationship. When my father told me of the Party's decision, I thought this would be the beginning of my new life. I quit the job and I told him not to bother me anymore. I thought I could erase that memory, but heaven did not allow it.

"Changsheng, if I had known I was pregnant, I would have told you the truth before the wedding. I would never deceive you. Please forgive me!"

Xiaohung was almost crying at the end of her confession. Yeh did not have the heart to watch a woman sobbing in front of him. He said:

"Xiaohung, I understand your situation. Let bygones be bygones!"

They did not talk to each other for a while. Then:

"Are you going to tell you parents about this?"

"No. They will kill me if I tell them. Changsheng, could you please keep this secret for me?"

Life grew back to normal again. No one mentioned this subject anymore.

One day in late August 1982, a colleague in the editorial office showed Yeh a news article in the *People's Daily* and asked Yeh whether he knew the U-2 pilots Yeh Changti and Chang Liyi. The news reported, "... Based on 'Revolutionary Humanitarian,' the Party Central (黨中央) approved the request of two KMT U-2 pilots to leave for Taiwan to visit their families. They were captured in the 1960s, released in the 1970s, and they were appointed as civil servants later." Any news published in *People's Daily* is an official announcement. It was good news to Yeh. However, after so many years living in this "proletariat dictatorship" country, Yeh knew he should not believe this was final. Any announcement could be changed. Not until he was actually standing on a place outside the jurisdiction of Communist China could he be complacent. He should not behave differently and he should not let his colleague know he was one of the U-2 pilots at this moment. He simply answered the question, "I don't know them."

The announcement was just made a week after the August 17, 1982, US-PRC Joint Communiqué on United States Arms Sales to Taiwan had been issued. The communiqué stated that the United States would reduce the sales of arms to Taiwan, and was regarded by the PRC as a great diplomatic victory on diminishing the tie between ROC and U.S., which was posted in *People's Daily* as top news and editorials. It seemed to Yeh that the timing of the announcement was well orchestrated to reap the maximum crop of psychological warfare. If that was the case, Yeh felt like being used as a pawn in the conflict across the Taiwan Strait.

The news revealed to him that he was not the only U-2 pilot captured in Communist China. As far as Yeh understood, five Chinese U-2s had been shot down over the mainland. Two pilots, Chen and Lee, were definitely dead. Chen's death was confirmed when Yeh was still in Taiwan. Lee must be dead too, otherwise the cadre would not have shown him the ring worn by Lee and asked him who the pilot was when Yeh was confined in the hostel in Beijing. No information had ever released to him about what happened to the pilots of the other two U-2s that had been shot down, one in Nei Mongol (Inner Mongolia) in January 1965 and one near Shanghai in September 1967. Chang Liyi must be one of them. The other one was most likely dead too.

Yeh remembered that he had met Chang Liyi several times in Taiwan while Chang was an F-100 pilot stationed in Chaiyi. Chang was three years his senior. He must have transferred to the Black Cat Squadron after Yeh executed his last mission, since he had not met Chang in that squadron.

Yeh told Xiaohung at lunch about the news. He also told her his real name. She said she still preferred to call him Changsheng. She seemed not to care that Yeh had been a U-2 pilot. She only understood that he would have a short trip to Taiwan soon.

Yeh started to prepare the teaching materials followed by the regular teaching work of the fall semester. The weather was getting cooler. Yellow chrysanthemums started to appear on campus. There was a basketball court near the faculty living quarters. In the early morning, many grown-ups came to the basketball court to practice Tai Chi Chuan. Some people followed the music played on a portable cassette player and danced as a morning exercise at one corner of the court. Yeh had never paid any attention to these activities since he moved to this apartment.

Xiaohung asked Yeh to join the dancing group. Xiaohung enjoyed ballroom dancing very much. She mentioned many times that all the high-ranking cadres enjoy dancing. Chairman Mao frequently held dancing parties in his residence before he died. Girls regarded being invited to participate in a Chairman Mao's dancing parties the utmost honor. To Yeh, the foxtrot or the waltz steps were already too old-fashioned even when he danced with Betty almost twenty years ago. The Mao suit worn by the dancers could not provide any sense of graceful motion. Xiaohung was so energetic that he could hardly catch up. Their nineteen-year age gap made so much difference both culturally and physically.

Cadre Xu came to tell Yeh in late September that the PLAAF decided to arrange a tour for Yeh and Chang Liyi to see all the great progress of China before leaving the mainland. Yeh should prepare to stay in Beijing for a few weeks after the first of October and he could bring his bride with him to have the tour together. Xu would accompany them to Beijing, for he had to take an official business trip there too.

Xiaohung was very excited about going with Yeh to Beijing, the place where she had had a short visit to rally praising Chairman Mao at Tiananmen Square in late 1966. In their eagerness to worship Mao, no Red Guard had ever thought about touring any scenic spot in the Beijing area, or complained about the unbearable accommodations and poor food. The disastrous experience of the crowded railway travel was a subject Xiaohung never liked to remember. This time was different. They were entitled to travel in the "soft seat" coach on a train, as Yeh was an associate professor. The associate professor was graded as fourteenth in the Chinese Communist civil service system, which was the lowest grade to buy upgraded railway tickets.

They could not tell whether it was because of the progress made in the past ten years or because the tickets were upgraded, but the "soft seat" coach was much more comfortable than that in which they had ridden many years ago. The aisle was not blocked by overbooked passengers. They could sit down to enjoy meals in a dining car.

They arrived in a PLA hostel in Beijing on the seventh of October. The cadre who received them introduced himself as Wang. He addressed Yeh as "Leading Cadre Yeh" (葉領導幹部) and addressed Xiaohung as "Comrade Ding." He said he was responsible for taking care of the room and board for them as long as they stayed in Beijing. He would also arrange transportation for them to visit other places. It sounded like a free-of-charge-package tour.

Chapter Eight: Jack's Miserable Story

Cadre Wang led them to a two-bedroom suite with a living room in between. The rooms all had private baths. There were no latches on the outside of bedroom doors like the "hostels" Yeh had inhabited eleven years ago. The furniture and interior decorations were much better, and there was no soldier on guard either. Wang told them in the living room:

"Leading Cadre, a soldier will deliver meals to this room for you. I will always be available; just call me by using the telephone on the table whenever you need me. Please feel free to use the hot water in the thermos bottle and the dry tea in the box to make your own tea, and enjoy the TV. I think you probably would like to have a rest after your long travel." Then Wang left.

The next morning, Major Chang "Jack" Liyi arrived. Yeh and Chang held hands and shook them for a long time to show how happy they were to see each other again. They did not know each other well. Yet they knew they were both U-2 pilots; they were both shot down by Communist surface-to-air missiles and captured by the PLLAF; they were both looking forward to leaving this hostile country, which had held them for so many years.

After Chang put his luggage in the other bedroom, they sat down in the living room to have long talk about each other's pathetic experience.

Chang had been selected to receive U-2 flight training at Davis Monthan AFB, Arizona, in the spring of 1964. Just a week after he reported to the Black Cat Squadron in July, one of the U-2s in the squadron was shot down over the mainland by the enemy. The whole squadron mourned the loss of another outstanding pilot. That was the third U-2 lost in a reconnaissance mission over Communist China in the past twenty-two months. He realized the danger of fulfilling his duty as a pilot in the Black Cat Squadron. However, he regarded the honor of being a U-2 pilot as worth the risk. The U-2 was the only aircraft in the whole world that could fly at almost twice the altitude of other modern jet aircraft. It could cover a distance of more than four times the range of an average fighter. It could collect intelligence that could never be obtained by any other means. The skill required to handle this aircraft, especially during landing, was the most difficult in the military aircraft inventory. Only the best pilots were selected to fly this spyplane.

He had his first photoreconnaissance mission over mainland China on October 31, 1964. On that mission, he took off from Takli AFB in northern Thailand, flew past Kunming toward Lanzhow, and then covered many targets on the way back to the home base at Taoyuan in Taiwan.

At about that time, the ChiComs tested their first atomic bomb, with destructive power equivalent to the American bomb exploded over Hiroshima, Japan, during World War II. It was suspected that the giant nuclear diffusion plants at Lanzhow and Paotow would produce higher-yield nuclear weapons. However, how soon they would achieve that goal depended on the process they were utilizing. Both the United States and the Republic of China in Taiwan were anxious to find out. It could be detected by using an infrared camera to measure the heat generated by the plants. However, the heat measurement had to avoid any interference of other heat sources or clouds. So a few night missions were planned and waited for clear weather over the target areas.

After the loss of Lee Nan-ping's aircraft, the CIA realized the radar warning receiver, System 12, was not sufficient to protect the U-2 from the attack of enemy surface-to-air missiles. They decided to install a deceptive radar jammer, System 13, on the aircraft, which was supposed to cause the target position shown on the enemy radar monitor to be inaccurate. System 13 was bulky and heavy. It took two external fuel tanks to carry. It might be the first passive radar jammer ever used in combat. Several missions had to be aborted because of the reliability problem of System 13.

On November 27, 1964, another U-2 pilot, Wang "Johnny" Shichuen, executed a night mission. When he flew close to the Lanzhow nuclear plant, multiple brilliant missile flames suddenly blinded him. The autopilot on board had helped him while he was recovering from temporary blindness. The missiles had obviously missed the aircraft. Although the mission was not totally success, the whole Black Cat Squadron felt fortunate and credited the System 13, which had made the missiles aim at a fictitious target and saved Wang's life.

Chang was assigned to carry out a night mission to the Paotow nuclear plant. This was his fifth mission penetrating the Bamboo Curtain. He had never expected that was his last mission. He told Yeh:

"Robin (Yeh's nickname in the Black Cat Squadron), you know my wife and three children were living in Tongkong, which was about six hours away from Taoyuan by train. I could only go home to unite with them on weekends. On Friday, January 7, Squadron Commander Yang told me not to leave that weekend, as the weather forecast over the target areas was improving. The mission could be dispatched anytime. I called my wife, Chaichi, and told her that I wouldn't be home until next weekend because of another engagement. I thought I would ask Yang for a few days' leave after that mission and go home to surprise her. I did not know that it would be the last conversation of our ten-year marriage."

The clear weather over the target areas finally arrived on Sunday. Wang flew the mission to Lanzhow on Sunday night. Chang was his backup pilot and would carry out the mission if for some reason Wang could not. Otherwise, the backup pilot helped with the preflight check and operated the "mobile" (command post on an automobile) until the aircraft came back and safely landed. Wang's mission was a success. He landed in Taoyuan AFB at 1:30 a.m. Monday morning.

Chang was scheduled to fly the mission to the Paotow nuclear plant in the night of Monday, January 10, 1965. He took a long nap after lunch and did some mild exercise then. After a brief physical checkup by the squadron physician, the squadron chef cooked a big T-bone steak, along with eggs and sides for his dinner, as always the meal for a U-2 pilot before a long mission. There was almost no way for the pilot to relieve himself, much less to discharge his waste, while wearing the pressure suit and squeezing into the narrow U-2 cockpit. The high-protein meal would eliminate the waste and provide long-duration energy.

He reported to the operations office two hours before the take-off time, as the routine procedure of U-2 mission required, to listen to the mission briefing about the objective of this mission and the hostile environment. Then he went to the personal equipment room to put on the pressure suit with the help of a specialist, and started to breathe pure oxygen for more than an hour to purge the nitrogen in his blood, which sometimes would cause pain in the joints of limbs at high altitude.

He took off from Taoyuan AFB at 6:30 p.m., cruised over the East China Sea, and checked System 13 to see if it was working. Then he pressed the microphone switch twice to notify home base that he was ready to penetrate the Bamboo Curtain near Shanghai. Upon reaching Qingdao, the command post at the Black Cat Squadron noticed that the single-side-band telemetry signals of the aircraft's operating condition, transmitted by Chang's U-2, became weaker and weaker, and were finally lost. Around 9:20 p.m., the ROC Communication Intelligence Station lost information on the U-2's position that they generally received by intercepting ChiComs air defense communications. The people at the command post could not figure out what had happened to Chang. They anxiously waited for Chang to contact his home base, until the estimated fuel remaining on board decreased to zero. The next day the ChiComs broadcast that another U-2 had been shot down.

Chang told Yeh what had really happened at that time:

"It was a beautiful night. The weather was magnificent. The good visibility made the new moon and the lights on the ground even brighter. Soon the new moon set in the west and the stars glistered in the sky. As I flew north, the snow reflection replaced lights over the rural ground. I did not find any contrail underneath my aircraft as we used to see during daytime missions over the mainland. That meant no enemy MiG was up to intercept me. The Communist jet fighters probably did not have the combat capability of interception at night. With the protection of System 13, I was confident I would complete the mission successfully. But confidence was not enough.

"When I had almost reached the target, a missile suddenly exploded nearby, with a blinding flash, breaking up the airplane. Neither System 12 nor System 13 had shown me any sign of warning in advance. I was thrown out of the cockpit and lost consciousness. I did not know how long I had been falling through the sky. When the jerk of the parachute automatically opening at about fourteen thousand feet above the ground woke me up, I felt excruciating pain on my right shoulder. The missile fragments must have pierced my flesh. My eyes were bloated, as if almost falling out of their sockets. The missile fragments must also have damaged the capstans or oxygen hose of my pressure suit, which caused the suit to momentarily fail to protect me from the thin air of high altitude.

"It was very difficult for me to tell how high I was in the air, as the flat ground was covered with snow or frost. Both of my ankles were severely sprained when I hit the frozen ground. Robin, you know the pressure suit we wore for flying U-2. There was no room for any kind of clothes under the tight suit except a layer of underwear, which certainly could not keep me warm in the subzero temperature. I pulled the parachute canopy close to me and wrapped myself in it.

"It was a totally different world. The earth was completely flat. I could not see anything above the ground but snow. It was a quiet that I had never experienced before. Time seemed to stand still. The monotonous surroundings hypnotized me. I felt like going to sleep. Yet I remembered the lessons we learned in the survival course, that we should not fall asleep in a very cold environment, to avoid being frozen to death. I should move around to keep myself awake, but my ankles prevented me from standing and walking. I could not find where I could seek help in the dark night. I did not know how long I would survive in this wilderness. I just lay down to save my energy.

"I did not know when and how long I had dozed off, but voices awakened me. In the direction of the voices I saw a group of people carrying torches. As they came near I could recognize they were carrying rifles too. From their conversation I understood they were obviously searching for me. I was getting too nervous and tried to lie as flat as possible on the ground and was glad the parachute canopy was white too. Fortunately, their searching path was not directly toward me. They passed me about one hundred yards away.

"As they moved away from me, I tried to get up to have some exercise to refrain from falling asleep again. I suddenly realized I did not have any feeling in my feet. The frostbite had attacked me. I thought the leather flying boots would keep my feet warm, but they did not. The thought of severe frostbite might necessitate amputating my legs to save my life made me doubt whether trying to avoid capture was a wise choice. I crawled around with my elbows and knees to stimulate my blood circulation.

"The dawn finally broke. In the twilight I saw a few yurts (Mongolian, portable, circular tents) over the horizon. I started to crawl toward the nearest yurt. It did not look very far, yet I crawled for a couple of hours to reach the yurt. The woman inside the yurt was very kind to me even though she recognized I must be the pilot of the KMT aircraft whom the militia had searched for the previous night. She let me stay near the fire in the middle of the yurt and told me not to warm my feet hastily. She gave me warm clothes and a woolen blanket, and provided a hot meal for my empty stomach."

After the meal she let Chang lie down on a bed. She wrapped his feet with a warm comforter and put a pillow under his feet to keep them elevated. She said this would help him to recover from the frostbite. Chang was grateful to her and would like to show his appreciation by giving her some RMB, which the U-2 pilot carried in the emergency kit on each penetration mission for buying his way out in case he was lost in the mainland. She looked at those RMB with a sneer and said:

"Comrade, you don't have to pay me for helping you. Besides, these are very old RMB. They had been out of circulation for many years."

Chang felt very much embarrassed and also unhappy about how the person responsible in the Black Cat Squadron could pack out of circulation money in the emergency kit. He threw that bundle of RMB into the fire. Anyway, Chang thought he had met a guarding angel. He did not know the woman was the wife of a production brigade commander of Shahaitze (沙海子) Commune. She had sneaked out to tell her neighbor to inform the local militia while Chang was taking his hot meal.

Militiamen came and took Chang to the commune office by donkey cart. Then, soldiers of the People's Liberation Army Air Force came to load him in a jeep and transport him to a military hospital about two hours away. They kept him in a special room with no other patients around. Interrogation started the next day and continued for quite a few weeks. Three months later, when Chang had recovered from his frostbite, shoulder wounds, and ankle sprain, he was transferred to a "hostel" near Beijing to be confined in solitary just as Yeh had experienced.

Chang was born in Nanjing, the capital of China when KMT was in control of the central government. When the Japanese invaded China in 1937, his family fled to Chongqing, just before the Japanese genocide of many hundreds of thousands of innocent Chinese in Nanjing.

Chongqing was the wartime capital of China, and became a main target for the Japanese Air Force. As the Chinese Air Force was weak, Japanese bombers raided Chongqing frequently almost without any resistance and dropped bombs indiscriminately, before the United States Air Force came to the rescue in 1942. People in that city had to spend much their time in the air-raid shelters during the daytime. Chang had his elementary education under those conditions.

After many years of fighting against the Japanese invasion, China became very poor. People were mostly undernourished. The Chinese Air Force could hardly find healthy adolescents qualified to be flying cadets. They established a high school, named Air Force Preparatory School, in a quiet rural area in western Sichuan Province and provided sufficient support to nurture candidates of capable military pilots. Chang went through a very tough screening and was accepted to enroll in that school.

His family moved back to Nanjing after Japan surrendered in 1945. Two years later, Chang followed his school to Taiwan, and lost contact with them after the Bamboo Curtain was erected.

In the interrogation the cadres told Chang that his mother and three siblings were still living in the mainland. They tried to use this relation to prompt Chang for more intelligence, even though Chang could not provide anything more than he knew. In return he asked to let his mother know he was here in the mainland and hopefully he could see her soon. He had not seen her for almost twenty years. The request was certainly denied. He did ask for the same permission many times whenever there was an opportunity during the five years' solitary confinement. The answers were always, "You should be patient. When the time is right, we will make arrangement for you to meet your mother."

On a warm spring day in 1970, the cadre came to tell Chang that a high authority had decided that Chang could go to Nanjing to unite with his mother and siblings for two weeks under one condition: he should not let anybody know he was a U-2 pilot. Then he would be transferred to a commune near Nanjing to learn Communism from the peasants. He was happy to learn of the impending change, but had no idea of how miserable life in the commune would be.

When Chang, accompanied by a cadre, walked into a dilapidated house, a group of people was already waiting there. They must have been informed of Chang's coming in advance. They were all residents of this house. Chang could hardly recognize who his mother might be among several old women in this group. Gray hair and deep wrinkles would certainly change the appearance of a lady. Chang's mother was also reluctant to show any emotion in front of the crowd, although she was surprised to see he had become so much different from the thirteen-year-old boy who had left home for the Air Force Preparatory School.

After a brief introduction to neighbors, Chang's mother led him to her home, which was just two connected rooms in the building. Chang's oldest brother, Kuching, was living with her. Kuching's wife had been sent to the so-called "May 7th Cadre School" in a distant countryside to have reeducation. She was only allowed to join her husband during holidays. Chang's other older brother, Lixien, was living on the other side of the Yangtze River, and his younger sister, Shuhui, was living in another city, all with their own families.

His mother told him how life had been and how his father had died. He told his mother how he was married and had his two sons and a daughter in Taiwan. There were so many things to talk about.

One evening, Lixien brought his family with him to see Chang. After talking about each one's life for a while, Lixien asked him:

"Did you ever hear my radio broadcasting?"

"What broadcasting?"

"About six years ago, our Propaganda Department told me to call you over the Central Broadcasting Station (中央台). Our Party told me to say, 'My dear brother, Chang Liyi, your mother and siblings miss you. We hope you can come back to your motherland. If you can fly back with your aircraft, you will be rewarded with eight thousand ounces of gold by our government.' I broadcast that message every week for quite some time. You had never heard of that?"

"No. We watched TV mostly whenever we had time in Taiwan."

"Then I was told to stop that broadcasting. I thought you must be for some reason not flying anymore. I was suspicious to think that you might have been killed in combat. I have never dared to mention this to our mother. Fortunately, that was not the case."

"Unfortunately, I was almost got killed."

"Anyway, we are very happy to have you back."

Chang did not continue the exchange. As to him, to reunite with his wife and children was more meaningful than to unite with his brothers, whom he only had a vague memory when he left for school twenty-eight years ago.

The commune where Chang was supposed to receive reeducation was located west of Nanjing, near the border between Jiangsu and Anhui Provinces. The difficult living conditions in the commune surprised Chang as being more or less like Yeh had experienced.

About three weeks after Chang reported to the commune, the commune Party secretary came to the evening meeting of the production brigade that Chang belonged to, and declared the beginning of the Dazhai (大寨) movement. The secretary had just returned from an official tour to the Dazhai commune in the barren mountain area of Shanxi Province. The eighty-three families of Dazhai commune dug into the hills to build terraced fields and subsequently became a prosperous community. The Communist Party secretary of Dazhai commune, Chen Yonggui, credited his success to "studying and creatively implementing Mao Zedong's thought." With the support of Mao's wife, Jiang Qing, Dazhai was named the national model of agriculture development. It was more proof of Mao's words, "Mankind can outsmart nature." She then ordered the whole country to study Chen Yonggui's published article and carry out "Agriculture learned from Dazhai."

The following several evenings, all the peasants in Chang's production brigade assembled to discuss how to learn from Dazhai. No one had any good idea how to "creatively implement Mao's thought" to increase productivity. The brigade leader finally decided to imitate Dazhai by building terraced rice paddies on some desolate hillsides. The extra work needed extra time to accomplish. He told the peasants, "From now on, we all work from dawn to dusk until the terraced fields are completed."

The labor was really physical torture for Chang. After so many years living in confinement without physical activity, the routine farm toil was already too hard on him. He was forty-one years old and did not have the strength of the younger ex-Red Guards who were under reeducation in the commune. He did not have the skill of a career farmer to save energy while completing the job either. The fifteen hours of continuous hard labor even deprived his time for recovering from exhaustion.

It was the harvest time of the first crop of rice. All the communes were required to pay half of the annual tax in grain based on the estimated production of that year. The commune Party secretary had boasted to his superiors that his commune would have a quantum leap in production that year by promoting the Dazhai movement. The tax that was supposed to be paid had increased accordingly. The grain left for the peasants was consequently much less than before. The Party secretary then ordered that all the people's food rations be reduced to 75 percent of the normal quantity, and promised to pay the difference back when the products of the terraced fields had been harvested. Chang told Yeh:

"It was really miserable. I had to feed myself with porridge instead of cooked rice as much as I could bear in order to save grains for the days to come. I had to endure hunger most of the time. No one dared to complain about anything to the Party secretary. His promises never materialized, because the terraced rice paddies project was a total failure. Without water up on the hill, we had to carry water to the terraced fields with two buckets and a bamboo shoulder pole to irrigate the crop. The newly cultivated rice paddies drank water faster than we could supply it.

"Many years later when Jiang Qing and her 'Gang of Four' were prosecuted, the truth finally came out. The whole Dazhai movement was a hoax. In addition to thousands of PLA soldiers stationed near Dazhai had built a thirty-mile-long irrigation system for the terraced fields, and the Party subsidized the commune with millions of RMB yearly. Chen Yonggui himself was an illiterate until forty-three years old. No one believed the published article was written by him."

The overburdened work and malnutrition gradually took its toll on Chang. He could not tell how much weight he had lost. He felt his steps were not sturdy as before. One day on the hillside he missed a step and fell down. He tried to use arms and legs to stop rolling down the slope. Both buckets of water sprayed all over him. He lay there to rest a while. When he tried to stand up, he felt severe pain in his back. He had to quit working and go back to lie down on his bed. The back pain was getting worse that night. He did not go to work for the next few days.

The team leader came to urge him back to work.

"*Lao* Chang, you should have enough rest. Get up and go to work."

"Leader, I still have pain in my back. I am afraid if I start to lift heavy things now, the back pain will never go away."

"You know you will lose ten work points a day this way. Get up to join the other people. If you cannot carry heavy things, I can assign you to do other work."

The so-called "other work" was to collect human waste from the latrines around the commune and the nearby towns. It was a dirty and filthy job. The stinky smell always drove decent people away. There was no other choice for Chang at that moment. From that day on, a wheelbarrow mounted with a wooden barrel and a long-handled ladle became Chang's companion. He pushed this cart leaving home every morning and returning when the barrel was full. Then he dumped the collected waste into a storage pit (to be used later as fertilizer) and washed the barrel and ladle for use the next day. As the days went by, the smell bothered him less and less; he thought this was not a bad job. He could rest as long as he liked along the way. He could reimburse a small amount of per diem for having lunch away from home.

Another New Year neared in 1973, it was the time to close everyone's work point account. Each work point had an official value. After deducting the expenses for rations and monthly allowances, the balance would be paid in RMB. If the balance was negative, the deficit would be carried over to the next year. Many peasants were angry about the records that the brigade leader announced to them in public. They suspected the leader had added many points to those who were loyal to him and slashed the records of those who opposed him. But, being illiterate or not having enough education, most of them could not calculate how many work points he or she had accumulated in that whole year.

After a lengthy argument, the dispute was finally settled by the order of the commune Chief to assign Chang to keep the work point records of the production brigade for the coming year. He was then released from the job of pushing the infamous wheelbarrow around. The new assignment was a pleasant surprise to Chang. He later understood that was all because he was the only educated outsider in that community.

Every late afternoon, Chang carried a roster and visited various places where people of the brigade were working. The team leaders would tell him how many work points should be awarded for the day's labor to each member of their teams. Team leaders always earned ten work points a day. He then systematically recorded the data on a register he designed. At the end of each month he posted the record on the walls of the meeting place. People could see their records clearly. Chang soon realized that the people in the commune gradually treated him more like a friend, not a class enemy anymore.

About the same time Yeh was released from Red Flag Commune, Chang transferred to a factory at Yuhuatai (雨花台), a suburb of

Nanjing. Beginning as an apprentice, he learned all kinds of trades in its machine shop.

He was happy to be closer to his mother. He could go to see her anytime after working hours. Chang's mother was living alone after Chang's brother, Kuching, reunited with his wife and moved to another city. One day in 1978, Chang's mother said to him:

"Liyi, I think you should get married again."

"Mother, you don't know how much I miss Chaichi and my three children. You know Chaichi and I had been together for sixteen years. I treasure every minute of being with her."

Chang had first met Chaichi in the summer of 1949, when they both were enjoying swimming in the clear water of the Pacific Ocean and enjoying the warm breezes over the white sand beach near Tongkong in Taiwan with friends. He was a cadet of the Air Force Academy. She was a fourteen-year-old high school girl. They both spoke with the Nanjing accent, as they had both been born in the old capital of China on the other side of the strait. They both had the same surname "Chang." They both had moved to Taiwan a year ago, just a few months before the Communists took over the mainland in 1948.

Chaichi soon introduced Chang to her parents. She was the only child in her family and Chang had lost contact with his parents. It seemed natural that Chang became a foster son of Chaichi's parents.

Seven years later they were married. At that time Chang was an F-84F fighter pilot stationed in Chaiyi; Chaichi taught elementary school near her parents in Tongkong. Chaichi's parents did not want their daughter to leave home, so Chang set his love nest in his in-law's house. Two years later the young couple's daughter was born, followed by their first son the next year. The old couple was happy about the family and became lively again with grandchildren running around. Their second son was only six months old when Chang was shot down over the mainland.

Chang's mother continued:

"I know you love her very much. But the world is cruel. After so many years, she might have remarried another person."

"But no one told me that she has definitely married again. Those cadres from the People's Liberation Army Air Force promised me many times that sooner or later they will let me go back to Taiwan. I had rather wait."

"After so many years you still believe they will keep their promises?"

"Mother, I am forty-nine years old now. I don't have the urge to make my life complicated again."

"Liyi, I am getting old. I don't think I will live forever. Who will take care of you after I am gone?"

Aging had been consuming her health steadily. Chang had to visit her more often, especially when she reached the hospice stage in 1979. He told Yeh:

"Ever since I was shot down over Inner Mongolia eighteen years ago, the only meaningful thing I had been allowed to do was to help my mother to go through the last phase of her life, to see her peacefully leaving this miserable world."

Chang did not continue to talk for a while. Both Yeh and Xiaohung did not disturb him either. Then he said:

"I think the Communist Party had been considering releasing us since 1980, because I was appointed to be an instructor in the Nanjing Aviation College (南京航空學院) that year without any reason. I was assigned to teach students bench work in the laboratory. By this appointment, I think they intended to show the world that they had treated prisoners of war well. In this country, propaganda is most important."

Time passed quickly, as they had much to talk about. The soldier brought in their dinner, and Cadre Wang came to tell them:

"Director of the PLLAF Political Department, Kuo Di, invited you all to have dinner in the Beijing Hotel tomorrow night."

"Beijing Hotel? Is it the famous hotel where President Nixon stayed when he visited China?"

"Yes! You are perfectly right."

"I was told that hotel only serves foreigners," Yeh said.

Wang did not respond to Yeh's comments; he just said, "I will request a Red Flag limousine to take you there around six o'clock tomorrow evening."

Yeh and Chang both knew Kuo Di very well. To both of them, he was the first cadre they met after leaving hospitals. He was now the director of the PLAAF Political Department. What a promotion!

Five U-2s of Black Cat Squadron had been shot down by Communist China. Four of them were displayed in front of the Military Museum, Beijing

Lost Black Cats

The U-2 piloted by Chang Liyi was shot down over Northern China. The pod on the left wing housed System 13, the radar jammer

Instructor Chang
Nanjing Aviation College 1982

Associate Professor Yeh,
Engineering College of the Central China, Wuchang 1982

Chapter Nine: Free at Last?

The eighteen-story Beijing Hotel was located along East Changan Avenue near Wangfujing (王府井) shopping street, about five minutes' walking distance away from Tiananmen Square in the heart of the business district. As the black Red Flag limousine approached the hotel, Yeh and Chang both realized that Beijing had drastically changed since they left there more than ten years ago. The streets were flooded with bicycles. People were not wearing only the blue-grayish baggy Mao suits anymore. Imported automobiles had replaced the horse carts. In the dusk twilight, no automobile had its headlights on. The cars drove the cyclists away by blowing their horns instead. The driver later told them he was concerned his headlights might blind oncoming cyclists. Twice traffic police stopped them on the way along with all the cyclists to let the siren-wailing military-style motorcades of imported black cars rush through.

Director Kuo's aide was waiting in front of the hotel when they arrived. He led them to a private dining room in the Noble Court at the lowest level. Cadre Xu was there already. The waitresses, wearing dark green, military uniform–like dresses, served hot tea and Zhonghua cigarettes, the best local cigarettes in China. Soon Kuo arrived with another cadre.

A large combo cold dish was placed on a lazy Susan at the center of the round table while Maotai liquor, the best spirits in China, filled all the small wine glasses in front of the eight people at the table. Kuo raised his wine glass and proposed a toast to welcome Chang and the Yehs. Then hot dishes followed, served one after another, with toasts in between. It was the greatest meal Chang and Yeh had had since they had involuntarily landed on the mainland. After a few rounds of toasts with the strong, white lightning liquor, they lost track of how many courses had been served. A big bowl of soup is always the last hot dish of a Chinese banquet. Kuo toasted Chang and Yeh again, and said:

"*Lao* Chang, *Lao* Yeh, I am very happy to be able to tell you that you can leave for Taiwan now. I know you have been looking forward to this permission for so many years. I hope you understand we could not treat the pilots of the world-renowned U-2 spyplane lightly.

"However, I still think you will have a problem uniting with your families. Do you remember that the *People's Daily* announced that Party Central had approved your request to visit Taiwan in late August? We have not received any favorable response from the Taiwan government since then. Our intelligence informed us that an official in the Taiwanese government had even said, 'Those two pilots will be court-martialed if they come back to Taiwan.'"

As a matter of fact, the Communist Chinese had guarded the secret of what happened to both U-2 pilots very well. No one in the free world could image that both of them were still alive so many years after their aircraft failed to return to their home base from their penetration missions. The public announcement in the Communist newspaper of their release must have caught the ROC government by surprise, and the government in Taiwan did not know how to respond.

Kuo's talk was a terrible shock to both pilots. They had risked their lives so many times to carry out the dangerous missions for protecting this island from Communist invasion. This was inconceivable to them, that the government in Taiwan would treat them so unconscionably. It could not be true! Should they believe what Kuo had said? Kuo was a veteran Communist cadre. Was it another act of psychological warfare? They just could not say anything at this moment.

Kuo continued, "In this case, we will send you to Hong Kong, the British colony. We know there is a Taiwan Liaison Office in Hong Kong. You will have to apply for Taiwan's entrance permit from there. *Lao* Xu will help you to obtain a six-month visa for staying in Hong Kong. If you cannot go to Taiwan within six months, you are always welcome to come back.

"Anyway, the Party would like you to learn more about the progress of this country before your going aboard. The Propaganda Department has a very good program to show you the accomplishments of this great nation. *Hsiao* Wang will take you there."

The food on the table was much more than the eight guests could consume. The leftovers were still piling up on the lazy Susan. A waitress served each guest a small bowl of sweet taro soup, a Chinese desert. It should be the end of this banquet. Chang and Yeh raised their wine glasses to thank Kuo for his hospitality. Kuo responded:

"You don't thank me. We all should thank our Party."

"We all want to thank you too. Because of your presence, we can have a reason to enjoy this wonderful meal," one of the cadres followed.

The banquet obviously was one of the fringe benefits for high-ranking cadres. They had a reason to enjoy good food. They had a reason to enjoy the luxury of wasting food, while people in other parts of the country remained on the verge of starvation. The banquet might cost more than several months' salary of the average person in China.

The next Propaganda Department program would start a week from next Monday. In the meantime, Cadre Wang took both pilots to a men's clothing store to have them measured for tailor-made Western-style suits, and to buy some shirts and ties. He also took them to a shoe store to buy real leather shoes. It was a big surprise to them. They had been wearing the baggy Mao suits and sneaker-like shoes for almost twenty years and never had enough money to consider buying any clothes of made wool. Wang told them that the Party did not want them to lose face when they arrived in Hong Kong.

A week later, the tailor delivered their wool suits. He proudly asked them to try them on and waited for some compliment from the customers. It must have been his first job of making Western-style suits. The suits looked like snugly tailored Mao suits. Both pilots thought they would really lose face if they wore them in Hong Kong. The suits were then returned for alteration several times until there was no further way to improve them.

One day Xiaohung wanted to buy some gifts for her parents. Wangfujing Street should be the right shopping place. Yeh and Chang accompanied her by bus. There were numerous shops along the pedestrian street, selling an uncountable number of merchandise, from antiques a few thousand years old to dresses of the latest fashion, from thingamajigs to sophisticated high-tech products. Among the huge variety of items, it was difficult for Xiaohung to decide on which was the right one to buy with her limited amount of spare money. They strolled from store to store until both fifty-year-old men felt tired. They went to a popular Beijing duck specialty restaurant nearby to have lunch.

When the flour patties, sweet paste, and scallion slices were on the table, and they all were waiting to taste the tender meat and the crispy skin of real Beijing duck, Yeh heard a familiar voice calling his name. It was Pan, his former roommate in the Red Flag Commune farm tool factory, who had just finished his meal with several friends and was walking toward the door through the aisle behind Yeh.

"*Lao* Yeh, it's very nice to see you. What makes you come here?"

"*Hsiao* Pan, what makes you come here too? I heard you were working in Guangdong (a province about two thousands kilometers south of Beijing)."

"It's a long story. Do you have time tomorrow? Where do you live in town? We should get together for a chat."

Yeh told him where he stayed. Pan said he would come to pick all three of them up the next day to enjoy an evening at a nightclub.

They were ready to have an evening meal in the hostel when Pan arrived. Pan looked at the food on the table and said, "Let's have a good dinner at the club."

Pan drove a very old, black Mercedes. But it was still a Mercedes, the most luxurious car in China. Yeh asked:

"A wonderful car! How long have you had it, *Hsiao* Pan?"

"Just about two months. You like it, don't you?"

From the way Pan drove and the way he shifted gears, everyone could tell that Pan had not had this car very long, nor had he been driving very long either.

"I heard that there were only twenty residents in Beijing that have private cars. You are one of them. You must be very successful," Yeh said.

"It was probably an old statistic. I would say the number of private cars exceeds one hundred now. Yet the number is still very small compared with the population in Beijing. Just one out of one hundred thousand people have a car," Pan replied proudly.

The nightclub was located on the second floor of a Friendship Department Store (the store especially set up for the foreigners). When they walked from a parking lot to the club, Pan made a few steps faster to talk to the plain-clothes police in front of the door. Then he waved his guests to follow him.

The club had a small stage at one end and a bar on the other end of the hall. Tables were laid out around, except the small area near the stage. A three-man band played popular music on the stage, and some people crowded on the small area to enjoy dancing. Under the dim lights and heavy cigarette smoke, Pan led them to occupy a table away from the stage. Then drinks and Western food were ordered.

Pan was most curious about Yeh's secret past. He said:

"I had long suspected that you were not an ordinary KMT officer after you moved to our room in 1972. When I read the news a few months ago about permitting two U-2 pilots to visit Taiwan, I was immediately sure that you were one of the two."

Then it was Pan's turn to tell his success story.

After graduation from the Engineering College of Central China, at Wuhan, Pan was assigned to work for a power company near Hong Kong. When the government announced it would set up two Export Processing Zones along the coast of Guangdong Province in 1979, Pan found a partner from Hong Kong and established a factory in Shenzhen to do the final assembly work of some small home appliances. His partner was responsible for a major part of the investment, the assembly technique, and sales. Pan was responsible for general management, especially dealing with the local Communist bureaucracy. Because of his father's influence, the bureaucrats did not cause them much trouble. The factory was an instant success. Part of the proceeds from exporting products was supposed to be exchanged for RMB in a government bank to pay for the operation and labor cost. Instead, he used that part of foreign exchange to import other merchandise, which was hot in the local market, then sold them for RMB to pay for the plant's operation expenses. He said:

"I soon found out there was great demand for TVs, refrigerators, and so forth. People were willing to pay any amount of money to buy them. It is all about 'supply and demand.' I could reap a profit several times more than I could earn from an export-processing operation. However, there was another kind of bureaucracy harassing the private business owners (個体工商戶). I was fortunate to have an influential father. Along with some hush money, business had been going very well."

Pan represented the quintessential member of the new nobility, which was generally called "children of high-ranking cadres (高幹子弟)." They were always leading the crowds in any movement. They were at one time the most dedicated Communist revolutionaries in the Cultural Revolution. Now they had become wholehearted capitalists.

Customers kept arriving until the nightclub was full. As the evening wore on, the revelers became tipsy, along with much flirting and laughing. Everyone seemed to enjoy very much the mesmerizing atmosphere. Singers from Hong Kong or other countries excited the audience with their seductive voices on stage. Some even stimulated them with dirty jokes. The swivel lights on the ceiling swept multicolor spotlights over the dancing crowds, revealing some young adults holding each other very tightly with sexy motions. It was a genuine picture of corrupted, decadent capitalists, which disgusted the Communist revolutionaries the most. How could this happen in this Communist country? The only excuse was this place was set up for the corrupted foreigners. Yeh noticed that there were not many Caucasians around. Most people in the club appeared to be Chinese. Maybe they were from other Asian countries. Maybe they were overseas Chinese. But many spoke fluent Chinese with authentic Beijing accents, especially those young females. He asked Pan:

"Are all the people here foreigners?"

"Definitely not. Many are friends of foreigners. Many have good connections. Some of them just have money to pay." He rubbed his thumb against his forefinger and middle finger to simulate counting banknotes.

"There are even some prostitutes brought in by the corrupted foreigners. I bet that girl is one." He pointed to a girl in a provocative dress.

Prostitutes! The word surprised Yeh even more. Ever since he was captured by the PLAAF, the cadres had always told him proudly that the Communist revolution had eliminated all the prostitutes and beggars in Chinese society. It now appeared right under the nose of the central government.

The program organized by the Propaganda Department was held in a conference room of the office compound, and was scheduled to run two weeks. Cadre Wang took them there on Monday morning.

It generally had a lecture in the morning, followed by a workshop to discuss what had been learned from the lectures, and a guided tour in the afternoon. There were about fifty participants. They were all dispatched to go abroad for various purposes. Some were assuming diplomatic positions, some pursuing further education, some exploring business opportunities, some involved in athletic competition, and some just visiting relatives. They all were excited, as this was their first opportunity to travel outside China.

In his opening remarks, the senior lecturer boldly told the participants:

"... You all should be grateful to our Party for the opportunity to go abroad. You should be aware that you are going to those countries having superficially a better material life, but full of poisonous thoughts. So we will arm you with correct thinking in this program...."

"Gosh! Another round of brainwashing!" Yeh thought.

The lectures covered all the achievements of the Communist Party. Many historical events, such as liberating tenant farmers from the abuse of landlords, liberating laborers from the exploitation of feudalistic capitalists, and many others, Yeh had heard many times before. He remained unconvinced that these events could be regarded as achievements. Yeh knew there were some other, better ways to achieve the same goals without hurting the whole country so badly. The KMT accomplished land reform in Taiwan without killing any landlords. Through unions, laborers could peacefully coexist with management in all the developed countries. There was no need to liberate laborers by confiscating businesses whose owners had spent several generations building. The lecturer said:

"Workers in the capitalist countries are badly exploited. Workers in China are working for themselves."

Yeh could not tell how good laborers were paid in Communist China. The laborers had no way to argue whether they had been paid appropriately based on their contributions. They just received what the government ordered. The laborers were not living better than the laborers in any of the capitalist countries. Yeh saw only Party officials living lavishly.

Some of the lectures were new to Yeh. The Party admitted that the three-year "Great Leap Forward" was a disastrous movement, and the ten-year "Cultural Revolution" caused even more damage to the country. The Party did not deny that Chairman Mao initiated both movements. But in spite of the mistakes he had made, Mao was still the greatest leader of the Communist world. With the leadership of the Chinese Communist Party and the administration of "proletariat dictatorship (無產階級專政)," Mao's teaching was the only theoretical basis for establishing a unique Chinese socialist country.

That afternoon a bus took all the program participants to pay tribute to the Mao mausoleum. Yeh remembered sixteen years ago that Tiananmen Square used to span from Tiananmen to the memorial of revolutionary martyrs. It now extended another two-thirds the length of original Tiananmen Square to the south all the way to the gate tower of Zhengyangmen. The old houses and trees between the memorial of revolutionary martyrs and Zhengyangmen had all been eradicated. The only architecture standing there was the huge, hollow vault of the Mao mausoleum. In the middle of the dimly lit hall there lay the corpse of Mao Zedong inside a glass casket, like a biological specimen of rare species kept inside a glass container filled with inert gas, with viscera removed and with preservative fluid injected. Yet people went through tight security and waited in a long line for a chance to bow down to that dead body. From the brief conversation with the visitors, Yeh understood all the visitors were peasants from distant provinces and dispatched by their local governments on official missions to visit the shrine.

The other afternoons, the participants of the program visited various historical or scenic spots: the Forbidden City, the Great Wall, the Summer Palace, the Ming tombs, etc. There were many places around Beijing that displayed the rich heritage of glorious Chinese history. There were also many places that displayed the accomplishments of the Communist Party: the Great Hall of People, the Museum of Chinese Revolution History (革命歷史博物館), the model school, the model factory, the model farm, and a reformed Beijing opera. They also visited the number-one machine tool factory at southeast of Beijing, which had about five thousand workers. Both Yeh and Chang noticed that living conditions in this factory were much better than in those factories they had worked for. The factory guide proudly told the visitors not how high their productivity had achieved, but the factory tradition of political correctness. He mentioned that during the Red Guard turmoil Chairman Mao ordered the factory workers propaganda team to clear the student chaos in Beijing University.

One of the mornings, the lecturer criticized at length racial discrimination in the United States, and praised the Communist way to treat the minorities in China. He did not mention that the treatment of Tibetans was not welcomed in Tibet, and their spiritual leader, the Dalai Lama, had fled to India. The lecturer also elaborated on the government's policy on reunification with Taiwan. He said the government had declared, "Under the sovereignty of the People's Republic of China, Taiwan would be able to maintain independent social, economic, and cultural relations with other countries as well as pursue a free-market economy, private property rights, and possess its own military. Leaders on the island can take up national posts." In other words, two independent political systems coexist in one country (one country, two systems 一國兩制). The first step toward the reunification would be direct trade (通商), direct transport (通航), and direct mail (通郵).

At the end of this indoctrination program, the minister of the Propaganda Department hosted a dinner for all the participants. Chang and Yeh were arranged to dine at the same round table with the host. The host told them during the meal that the KMT government in Taiwan had rejected the reunification offers and refused to consider direct trade, transport, and mail. He asked for their opinions on this subject. They really had nothing to say. First, they had only heard one side of the story. Second, if everything the host said was true, the KMT government must have its reasons for rejecting the offers.

At the end of the dinner, the minister addressed all of the guests. "… When you arrive in a foreign country, don't forget you are representing your motherland. Many of the countries are prejudiced against socialism. They don't appreciate what our great leaders have done for our country. You have the responsibility to propagandize our government policy.…"

It sounded as if everybody at dinner had completely agreed with the government policy without the slightest doubt. Everybody arriving in a foreign country should automatically become a member of the PRC government propaganda team. Maybe it was only natural in this Communist country where every piece of land belonged to the government; every school, factory, hospital, temple, service agency, retail store, even entertainment facility was owned by government. The whole one-billion-plus population, except for a few private business owners, was all working for the government. So they were all government employees. Thus, they should have the responsibility to carry out the government policies.

Cadre Xu came to tell both pilots he had acquired Hong Kong visas for them, and they would be permitted to go there now. However, the minister of the Education Department and the minister of the United Front Department (統戰部) would arrange farewell dinners for them before leaving Beijing. Both Ministers were busy men. Both pilots had to wait patiently.

At the dinner hosted by the minister of the United Front Department, the host mentioned the "one country, two systems" policy again. He denounced the stubbornness of the KMT government in rejecting direct contacts. He authoritatively asked both pilots to speak for this policy when they arrived in Taiwan. Yeh suddenly realized their release from the mainland was not only for the reason of "revolutionary humanitarianism" to unite families. They were being used to carry out the Communist government's Taiwan policy also.

On a crisp morning in early November, Cadre Xu accompanied Chang, Yeh, and Xiaohung to board an airplane leaving Beijing for Guangzhou in southern China, where they would stay in a hotel overnight and catch a train the next day to Shenzhen, the border town next to Hong Kong.

Yeh and Xiaohung talked about their future many times when they were alone. There was no clear picture what would happen after Xiaohung saw Yeh off in Shenzhen at the Hong Kong border.

If Yeh returned to Taiwan and settled down there, Xiaohung wished to join him. The life in Taiwan was much better than that on the mainland. Even the Communist government acknowledged the difference in living standards across the Taiwan Strait. The government had declared, "Learn economy from Taiwan (經濟學台灣)." But whether the Communist government would allow Xiaohung to leave the mainland was a big question. Otherwise, the Party would have not bothered to arrange their marriage.

If the Taiwan government refused to let Yeh go back to unite with his parents and siblings, as Director Kuo had told him, he would be very disappointed, and would have no other choice but to go back to Wuhan to rejoin Xiaohung. And yet if he were allowed to go Taiwan, it would be doubtful whether the Taiwan government would permit him to return to Communist China again.

Anyway, Yeh would leave all his savings to Xiaohung, and she could live on Yeh's salary, as they understood that the school expected Yeh would be back. Xiaohung told him she would keep Yeh's apartment, yet she herself would move back to live with her parents to wait for him. She also said:

"Changsheng, you know what I will do after I get home? The first thing I would like to do is to find a doctor to help me have an abortion. So when you come back, we will have our own child."

"Do you think it is safe to have an abortion?"

"I think so. It is quite common nowadays. Since the government declared the 'one child' decree in 1978, besides contraceptives, abortion is the only way to strictly follow the regulation that every family have only one child"

"I think you still have to consult a good doctor." Yeh looked at her expanded waistline.

The train arrived at the border station in the afternoon of November 10, 1982. A short distance from the station, there was a bridge spanning a river, which crossed the border between mainland China and the British colony of Hong Kong. A gatehouse stood on the Chinese side of the bridge.

After Yeh and Xiaohung said good-bye to each other and promised to keep in touch by letters, Yeh followed Cadre Xu and Chang to the gatehouse. Upon reaching the gatehouse, Xu said to both pilots:

"*Lao* Chang, *Lao* Yeh, I have to say good-bye now. I cannot go into the gatehouse. In the gatehouse, the officials will check your travel documents. Then you will be allowed to cross the bridge to the Hong Kong side. After the Hong Kong police check your visas, a travel agent named Pei from the China Travel Agency will come to meet you. He will take care of you while you are in Hong Kong."

Xu then said to Yeh: "Don't worry about your 'lover.' I will accompany her all the way back to Wuhan." He shook hands with both pilots, bade them good luck, and walked back to the railroad station.

It was a busy border-crossing gate. There were quite a lot of people leaving Communist China for Hong Kong, and vice versa. Chang and Yeh waited in line to go through the checkpoints. Many of the people in line spoke the Guangdong dialect and carried Hong Kong passports, doubtless Hong Kong citizens returning from business trips in China. Some of them spoke Taiwanese. Yeh curiously asked one of them:

"Are you from Taiwan?"

"Yes, why?"

"Did you have a nice trip over the mainland?"

"Fairly good. I visited my grandparents, whom I had never met before."

"Where are you going next?"

"Back to Taiwan."

"Then why do you have to go to Hong Kong?"

"You don't know we have to go through a third country to visit the mainland? The government in Taiwan would never issue me a passport if I told them I planned to go the mainland. The mainland government does not accept the Republic of China's passport either. So, I had to come to Hong Kong to apply for an entrance permit to the mainland at the PRC consulate there. I have to go through the same procedure for going back to Taiwan. In fact, my grandparents' house is only ten miles west of Quemoy (an island under ROC government jurisdiction). But I have to endure all this trouble to reach there."

Yeh suddenly realized that after so many years there still existed a non-negotiable gap between both governments, in spite of the fact that people on both sides of the straits used the same language and shared the same traditions.

Several men in military uniform checked both pilots' documents and personal belongings in their small bags. They were then directed to go through the gate to step onto the bridge.

As they walked slowly away from the PRC soldiers in grass-green uniforms and red collar insignia, holding rifles at the gate, and the five-star red flag waving in the air on top of the gatehouse, both pilots felt a sense of relief. It was the first time, since they were captured by the PLAAF, they did not have to worry that some unintentional comments might be recorded in their dossiers and used against them when the political winds changed. They would not be called to attend meetings to make self-criticisms or to read the Party's indoctrination, which they could not care less about, yet they were required to interpret and to discuss how to implement them.

They stopped momentarily over the middle of the river to enjoy the feeling of "free again." On the other end of the bridge there stood several Hong Kong police wearing khaki uniforms with pistols hanging at their waists. The double-red-cross-over-blue flag floating in the wind over the gatehouse pointed out it was British territory.

Although Yeh had lived there in his childhood, he felt the place was so foreign to him, for he did not know what kind of fate awaited him there.

Chapter Ten: Ordeal in Hong Kong

Perhaps because their clothes were different from the other people entering, or perhaps because their permits to stay in Hong Kong for six months were rare, but the clerk in gatehouse checked Chang's and Yeh's travel documents very carefully. The clerk even called his English supervisor to review them once more. The other clerk dumped everything out of their small bags to find out if there was any illegal substance. Then they were allowed to leave the gatehouse through the door on the other side. A young man in his early thirties approached them, introduced himself as Pei, and led them to board another train to go to the hotel.

Their hotel, with the name of International House, was located at Nathan Road in Kowloon near Victoria Harbor. After checking in at the registration counter, Pei accompanied them to their room. He told them the travel agency would pay the hotel bill. The agency was also authorized to provide them living expenses while they were in Hong Kong. He gave them each twenty-four hundred Hong Kong dollars (close to twelve U.S. dollars a day) for the first month per diems. He also gave them his address and telephone number and said:

"If you need help, please contact me any time."

"You probably know why we came here. Do you know where the Taiwan Liaison Office is located?" Chang asked.

"I know they have an office somewhere. I don't know the exact place. Let me find out and I will call you." Then he left.

There were two twin beds and a private toilet in the room. The interior decoration and furniture were quite shabby. Chang and Yeh noticed the neighbors seemed all to be from mainland China, as they all spoke Mandarin, not the Quangdong dialect or English, as the people in Hong Kong did. They understood that the Chinese Travel Agency was definitely a PRC government organization, as was every other organization in mainland China. They suspected this hotel was owned by the PRC too, or at least had a very friendly relationship with the PRC. There might be some Communist secret agents in this hotel too. They still had to be cautious.

Pei called them the next day to tell them the address of the Taiwan Liaison Office, which was located on the Hong Kong Island. Pei also told them that they should each prepare two photos for applying for entrance permits. The next day they put on their only Western-style suits and walked down to the Victoria Harbor to catch a ferryboat to Hong Kong Island.

At the liaison office they filled out the application forms for entrance permits. The clerk looked at their rustic suits for a while, then reviewed the forms and photos and said:

"Come back a week from today. The permit should be ready at that time."

There seemed to be no problem returning to Taiwan, and they looked forward to claiming their permits. In the meantime they shopped around to buy clothes that average Hong Kong people wore. They did not want to be recognized as from the backward rural country.

A week passed, and they went to the liaison office. The clerk greeted them and said:

"Would you please wait for a while?" She went to the back office for a while and came out with a gentleman. The gentleman said politely:

"Mr. Chang and Mr. Yeh, we are very sorry. Your applications have been rejected by our government."

"Why?" They asked almost in unison.

"I don't know why. We were just told to do so. We are very sorry!"

They were extremely disappointed, but not desperate. As they learned from the local newspaper that Chiang Chingkuo was now the president of the Republic of China in Taiwan. Chiang used to be the top supervisor of the U-2 US-ROC joint project when Yeh and Chang were pilots of the Black Cat Squadron. Chiang had visited the squadron and talked with the pilots frequently. He had hosted many dinner parties for both American and Chinese members of this squadron. He knew how difficult U-2 missions were and how courageous the pilots were. If Chang and Yeh could find a way to reach him, there should not be any problem getting back into Taiwan.

As they walked back from the ferryboat toward their hotel on Nathan Road, they met a group of the China Airlines crew in front of the Imperial Hotel. One of the crew, wearing a captain's uniform, looked so familiar to Chang. Chang just could not resist approaching him, and said:

"Are you Li Chingyueh?"

Li was his classmate in the Air Force Preparatory School and the Air Force Academy. They had worked together in the F-84 fighter squadron for several years.

The captain stared at Chang speechless for a while, and then said.

"It's impossible! Could you be Chang Liyi? We all know that you were shot down over the mainland. Our Air Force declared you died in that mission and built a tomb in the Air Force cemetery for you many years ago. How come you are here?"

"Yes, I am Chang Liyi. It's a long story. Do you have time?"

"We are on the way to the airport to fly the next hop. Don't worry. I will be back soon. Hong Kong is a regular stop of the course I am flying now. Where can I reach you?"

Chang told him his room number in the International House hotel. Li added:

"By the way, Liu Jetchuang will land in Hong Kong day after tomorrow. Do you remember Liu? He is now a captain of Far East Airlines. I know he is scheduled to fly a charter flight to come Hong Kong. I will tell him your address." Then the crew members boarded a bus and left.

Both China Airlines and Far East Airlines were companies in Taiwan. Liu was another classmate of Chang's. After graduation from the Air Force Academy, Liu had been assigned to a fighter squadron in Pingtung. Chang was sent to the United States to learn how to fly F-84F. Not long before Chang undertook his last U-2 mission, he was informed that Liu had been selected to join the Black Cat Squadron too.

It was late afternoon when the telephone in Chang's room rang.

"May I talk to Mr. Chang Liyi?"

"Speaking."

"I am Liu Jetchuang. I am at the Imperial Hotel. May I come over to see you right now?"

"I think it's better to meet you at your hotel. It only takes five minutes to walk to your place."

"Then, I will wait for you in the hotel lobby."

Chang and Yeh met Liu in the hotel. They were all U-2 pilots. They had much to talk about. Liu invited them to have dinner together. Chang and Yeh told Liu their miserable experiences in mainland China and their present situation. Liu told them his life after being selected to fly U-2s. When he completed his training in Tucson, Arizona, and came back to Taiwan to join the Black Cat Squadron, Chang and Yeh were lost over the mainland. He started his overflight missions in July 1965. He was very fortunate to complete ten missions over the mainland without any incident, and then was released from U-2 duty. He later was assigned as commander of the Black Cat Squadron from 1970 to 1972. Then he retired from the Air

Force to become an airline captain. He also told them the Black Cat Squadron disbanded in 1974.

Chang did not have the patience to wait long and asked Liu anxiously, "Do you know my wife, Chaichi? Could you tell me how she has been doing all these years?"

"I don't know much about her. I think she is working for China Airlines now. You must know Gimo. Gimo is now a captain at China Airlines. He should know your wife very well. I will tell him your situation and ask him come to see you after I've returned."

Yang "Gimo" Shihchu had been the deputy commander of the Black Cat Squadron when Yeh was working there. He was later promoted to be the squadron commander when Chang was in that squadron.

The next important subject they discussed was how to let President Chiang know the wishes of these long missing pilots. They decided to write a joint letter to the General Kuo Julin, Commander-in-Chief of the ROC Air Force. General Kuo had chances to see President Chiang personally. Liu helped them finish the writing and planned to carry it back Taiwan himself.

It was almost midnight when they left the Imperial Hotel. Liu said to them:

"Both China Airlines and Far East Airlines have contracts with this hotel. All our crew will stay in this hotel when they stop over Hong Kong. I think you can always find some airline crew from Taiwan in this hotel. Many of the airline pilots are our schoolmates. If you need any help, don't hesitate to come find someone to help you or ask someone to tell us your needs."

The words were so nice and warm. Chang and Yeh were glad to have finally found some friends they could rely on after so many years.

A week later, Gimo arrived. Chang and Yeh went to the Imperial Hotel to meet him. They were very happy to see their old boss again. The Black Cat Squadron only had a few pilots. Because of the dangerous missions they flew, pilots, including the commander and his subordinates, were very close.

Gimo told them the letter they wrote had been sent to General Kuo's office. He requested to have an appointment with General Kuo concerning this matter. Gimo and Kuo had worked for the same fighter squadron for some time when they were still young. But Kuo refused to see him. Gimo said to them:

"Jack (Chang's nickname in the Black Cat Squadron), Robin, don't worry too much. All our schoolmates are willing to help you. We have other connections to reach high levels of government. I will continue to ask them to push for a favorable response. But it may take time. You both have to be patient."

He told Chang that when his wife, Chaichi had received word that Chang was released and in Hong Kong; she immediately sought to obtain a passport and a Hong Kong visa. Gimo said:

"I estimate she will be here in ten days. It has been almost eighteen years since you went missing. Eighteen years is a long time. Many things have changed. I think it's better to let her tell you how she has been doing in these many years. I can only tell you that your daughter, Tsingyi, graduated from Taiwan University, the best university in Taiwan the last summer. She is now applying for graduate education in the United States. Your older son, Chingyi, is now a senior in another university. Your other son, Luke, is studying in a high school," Gimo continued:

"Robin, your parents are still living in Taiwan. Your brother immigrated to the United States last year after retiring from the ROC Air Force. You know that your brother and I are close classmates. I lost contact with your wife, Betty. She moved to the United States many years ago."

"Gimo, a cadre had told me many years ago that she had remarried."

"I heard that too. But I didn't know whether I should tell you that or not."

The next few days were very tough for Chang. He was so anxious to see Chaichi again. Yet he did not know how to receive her. He did not know how to treat a woman who had been so intimate with him long ago. He looked at the gray hair near his temples in the mirror and hoped that age had not left its marks on Chaichi's appearance. He wondered whether Chaichi would still look at him, dressed in these shabby clothes, with affection.

The expected phone call finally reached Chang. He rushed to the Imperial Hotel to meet Chaichi. She arrived with another female employee of the China Airlines. After a brief introduction, the other lady left them alone in a booth of the hotel coffee shop.

"Liyi, I always had a hunch that you are still alive, not like what the Air Force told me. I am so glad the Communists finally let you go. Our daughter and sons are all grown-ups now."

"Gimo has told me that. I believe it was very difficult for you to bring them up. I am very sorry for not being able to help."

"Are you married?"

"No. Why do you ask this question?"

"You had never married anyone all these years?"

Chang did not reply, as he sensed instinctively something might not be what he had hoped. A moment of silence later, Chaichi continued:

"If you had married in the mainland, I would have a less guilty conscience now."

Then Chaichi told him about her life after the last phone call they had on the first Friday of 1965.

It was noontime of Tuesday; she rode her bicycle from school to have lunch at home. She saw several Air Force officers standing in front of her apartment. She immediately sensed something must have happened to her husband, as she remembered Chang had told her on the phone last Friday that he would not come home for the weekend because of some other engagement. She knew that he was going to carry out a military mission, even though he did not tell her.

Inside the apartment, General Hsu Huansheng, Commander-in-Chief of the ROC Air Force was comforting her sobbing parents. General Hsu said:

"Major Chang did not return from the mission over the mainland last night. We don't know what actually happened to Major Chang at this moment. No matter what happened to him, the Air Force will take care all of you. Please let me know whenever you need help."

Two months later, the Air Force announced that Chang should be categorized as "died in line of duty," and built a tomb for him in the Air Force cemetery in Pitan, Taipei. Chaichi was invited to participate in the memorial service for all of the pilots sacrificed in that year, on March 27 of 1965, the Youth Day, a national holiday in the Republic of China.

She lost enthusiasm to teach the children in school. Most of the time, she held her baby son, thought about the happy times she had had with Chang, and wept occasionally. Her parents decided that a change of environment would be helpful. With the help of General Hsu, she was employed as a bookkeeper in the financial section of China Airlines. Then the whole family was moved to a compound for Air Force officers' families in Taipei.

Friendly colleagues in her office and sympathizing neighbors in the compound soon helped Chaichi regain her vitality. With her parents' help, the working single mother devoted herself to raising her three children. Nine years later, she was almost forty years old. Her children were still in school. Her aging parents needed help instead of helping her; friends introduced her to a compassionate bachelor, an army colonel named Ho Chungtsun. Several months later, Ho proposed. Chaichi refused to accept, as she still believed Liyi was alive. Ho finally said: "If Chang would come back to Taiwan, I would leave the family anytime as both of you wish, without any argument."

Chaichi told Chang:

"Before I planned to come to meet you, I asked Ho whether he would keep his old promise. He answered affirmatively."

Chang should have not any resentment. Although there were wrinkles at the out corners of her eyes and some additional weight around her waist, Chaichi was still the resilient, lovely women he used to know. Although she was now someone else's wife, there was still hope for him. If he could get back to Taipei, he would resume family life with his wife and children.

Chang told her of his life on the mainland. Chaichi told him all the reminiscences about their three wonderful children, in addition to showing him their photos. This was her first trip to Hong Kong. Chang wanted to take her to see the city and take advantage of this famous shopping place in the Far East. Anguished, Chaichi had no mood to enjoy any of them. She caught an early flight back to Taipei next morning.

A month passed. Pei came to give them the per diems for the next month and asked about their applications for entrance permits to Taiwan. They told him the applications were rejected and they were working to obtain them through other channels. Pei said:

"Do you need any help? I have a friend who works for the Hong Kong branch of the Xin Hua (New China) news agency. If you like, I can ask him to publish articles to exert some media pressure on the KMT government."

"Thank you for your offer. We think it's too early to consider that."

After Pei left, Chang and Yeh said to each other that both of them should be very careful in dealing with this offer. Otherwise they would be used as an instrument by the Communist government to denounce the other government globally. Even though they refused the offer, a reporter came to see them the next day.

"Mr. Chang and Mr. Yeh, I am Zhao. *Lao* Pei told me your situation I think I can help you. Don't you believe 'the pen is mightier than the sword'?"

"Mr. Zhao, thank you very much for your thoughtfulness. But we think it is too early to publish an article about that."

"I think you know the situation better. But on the other hand, your unique experience is a very good subject to report. I can write a book about how Mr. Yeh successfully went through 'learning from peasants and labors' and self-education to become a professor. The best time to publish this book is when Mr. Yeh returns to teach next semester in February. It takes time to write a book and also have to have many interviews. Could we start the interview sometime next week?"

Who told him that I would return to Wuhan to teach next February? Yeh was astonished and said so to himself silently. So far he had received two letters from Xiaohung. Both letters mentioned that the school wanted him to resume teaching after the Chinese New Year. The second letter mentioned the school would withhold his salary until he came back, so she had to find a job for herself. Xiaohung did not mention anything about abortion. She must have decided not letting the Party know their private matters, as it was an open secret that all international mail would be inspected by some security agency in Communist China. It was obvious that even in Hong Kong he was still monitored by the Party functionaries. He had better not disappoint the reporter Zhao.

"Thank you for your offer. Could you let me read it before sending it for publication?"
"No problem."
"In this case, please give me a call before you come to have an interview."

One day Yeh was very surprised to receive a letter from Betty's sister, Hsiaotung. She was preparing to leave from the United States, where she resided, to visit her parents in Taiwan and planned to make a stopover in Hong Kong for a few hours. She would like to meet Yeh at the airport. It was very good news to Yeh, as Hsiaotung was the one who introduced Betty to Yeh at the very beginning of their romance. Yeh could expect to find out Betty's situation from her.

When the scheduled flight arrived at the airport, Yeh held a cardboard sign high with the conspicuous name "Hsiaotung" on it and waited at the exit gate of that flight. Soon he saw someone waving at him. Yeh was happy that he did not miss her. They had not seen each other for almost twenty years. Age had changed their personal appearances.

They sat down in a restaurant. Hsiaotung handed him a package from Betty. She told him Betty was married, which Yeh knew already, and had two teenager boys. Her husband was teaching at the University of Rochester, New York. Yeh did not open the package from Betty immediately, not wanting to show his emotion in public, in case he found some sentimental things inside. He asked Hsiaotung how she had learned his address. She replied:

"You must know Deng Xiaoping, the leader of Communist China. He has a son, Deng Zhifang, who is now pursuing a Ph.D. in the University of Rochester. Betty's husband happened to be his major professor. Deng Zhifang frequently provided his professor with the *People's Daily*, the official newspaper of Communist China. So Betty sometimes had the chance to read these outdated newspapers. She found the news about your release by the Communists. She called me and asked me to find out your situation from the PRC consulate in Houston, where I live. They gave me your address just recently. Then Betty and I planned this trip."

Hsiaotung told him about her family situation, and that almost all her siblings and their families were living in the United States. They were planning to move her parents there too. Yeh told her about his life in the mainland and his Party-arranged marriage. Then Hsiaotung said:

"Betty and I are both willing to help you. Please let us know whatever you need by phone or letter."

After Hsiaotung left, Yeh stayed in a quiet place and opened the package. Inside he found a long letter, a stack of U.S. banknotes, and a stack of photos. In the letter, Betty told Yeh the terrible time she went through after the Air Force announced that Yeh was missing and then said he had died in his mission. Many male pursuers presumed the young widow understood male physical attraction. Even her boss, a married man, tried to make passes at her. She had to quit her job. Her mother frequently expressed her sorrow for Betty and regretted that she had not been persistent enough to prevent

Betty from marrying a fighter pilot. Finally Betty decided to join one of her sisters in the United States and seek opportunities for further education. Then a friend introduced Professor Huang to her. His wife died a year earlier, with no children. Professor Huang's sincerity made her agree to marry him.

She also wrote in her letter: "… I understand that the living standard in mainland China is much inferior to that in Taiwan. You may need money to start your life there. Hopefully, the enclosed two thousand dollars will help you for a while. If you need more please let me know.…

"… I always think the time we were together is the best part of my whole life. We enjoyed each other's company. We shared dreams. We were never bothered by daily chores. We never thought the world would be cruel like this. So I always carefully keep our photos in a safe place near me. I made a copy of them after I learned you were released from Communist China. I enclose them in the package and hope you will treasure them as I do.…"

Tears filled Yeh's eyes. He could not continue reading the letter or reviewing the photos. Yet he felt warm-hearted. Betty had not forgotten him, even though her husband and two lovely teenagers must now surround her. Yeh had his own wife waiting for him on the mainland too. This was just fate. No one can change his or her fate. He packed up the package after he had calmed down, and left the airport for his hotel.

Another month passed. No friends from Taiwan who stayed overnight in the Imperial Hotel brought them any favorable news. The Chinese New Year was near. People along the streets seemed busier in preparing for the most celebrated festival of the year. One day Gimo called them and asked them to come over to his hotel.

"Jack, Robin, I have finally got an answer from the government. You will be treated according to a newly authorized regulation: 'All military personnel captured by the Communists must stay in a third country for more than five years before applying for an entrance permit.'"

"What? We only have the permit to stay in Hong Kong for six months. How can we find another country to let us stay for five years?"

"I thought about this too. So I called Russ. You both must remember Russ. He was the American U-2 pilot in the Black Cat Squadron. His real name is Bob Ericson. He is now retired from the CIA and living in California. He and I have kept in touch all these years. I called him and asked him whether he could contact some his old acquaintances to request assistance for you. He said he would try his best. He said he needed your personal letter to work with. In these letters you should state your situation now and your intention of staying in the United States. Do you want to live in the United States for five years?"

"This is probably the only way available to us now."

They started to draft the letters immediately in order to let Gimo personally carry these letters to Russ in the United States. Then Gimo said:

"I have to warn you not to have too much hope on this. You know the Black Cat Squadron was disbanded eight years ago. We are not supposed to admit having had relations with the CIA openly. After so many years, that the CIA would openly help you is very doubtful."

"We can only 'treat a dead horse as if it were alive' (死馬當活馬醫), as the Chinese saying goes. But I don't understand why the government treats us in such an inconceivable way. Have they all forgotten that we risked our lives to collect intelligence for the defense of our country?" Chang said.

"It is all politics, all bureaucracy. One channel told me that the government had paid all of funds for the relief of families of those who had died on missions. They had built tombs for them at the Air Force cemetery. They had taken care of the survivors. To them the case is closed. The officials don't want to reinvestigate who made the wrong decision. The other channel said that you were all appointed professors at the Communist universities. They don't believe you could have been appointed to these positions without having been thoroughly brainwashed. Who can guarantee that you are not coming to Taiwan to carry out some secret mission for the Communists? Someone even said, 'The Communists have kept knowledge of your life or death a secret for that many years and now that they have suddenly released you with good physical condition is a pure scheme of psychological warfare. We just cannot allow you coming back and spreading the word about how well you have been treated by the Communists, with the intention of weakening the fighting will of our Defense Forces. ...'"

"I just don't understand why our return is so terrible. No one bothered to ask us what we really think about the Communists?"

"I don't think you should feel bad about this," Gimo added. "You know when Gary Powers, the captured American U-2 pilot, was released in February 1962 by the Soviet Union after twenty-one months' detention, many ranking officials were hostile to him. Many of them suspected Powers had revealed operational secrets to the enemy. After eight days of detailed investigation, including a polygraph, he still could not win recognition for what he had sacrificed for his country. Based on the limited information released by the investigation, the media painted a very negative image of Powers, until the CIA finally awarded him with an Intelligent Star three years later, in April 1965."

A few days later, Yeh received another letter from Xiaohung in China. This was her fifth letter. She urged Yeh to return as soon as possible. She wrote, "... My father said, 'Don't waste time on waiting for a KMT government's permit. Here we have many good opportunities for you. Our government is now organizing political party councils (政協會) to keep constant communication between the CCP and various small parties. If you are not satisfied with being an associate professor, I can maneuver through my connections to let the government appoint you as a council member (政協委員) representing neo-KMT (國民党革新委員會, a gathering of KMT members left in the mainland), which will be compensated at least as a Grade 8....'"

The associate professor was Grade 14 and received a compensation of two hundred RMB a month, an exceptional wage in a society where the average salary was around sixty RMB a month. Grade eight would certainly make life better. Should Yeh give up the hope of reuniting with his parents?

To go back to the mainland meant giving up his personal privacy. Besides, no one could be sure how long the recent political progress would continue. During those years Yeh lived under PLAAF surveillance, he had seen political turmoil many times. The whole country had a very unstable political system. The Communist Party controlled both the legislative and the judiciary functions. They could quickly change laws and interpret them as they wished. The top-ranking officials of the executive branch were all Party members, appointed by the Party. Why did the country have to be solely led by the Communist Party? What does "proletariat dictatorship" mean? Those functionaries in power had no longer been proletariats anymore. They lived in luxury like rich capitalists. Anyway, there were no "checks and balances" in the basic structure of the whole political system. The chairman of the Party had unchallenged power, and most probably would be corrupted before long by his excessive power. He could easily turn the whole country upside down at his discretion any time. The country would never be stable. Yeh decided not to go back, at least at that moment. He replied to her that he still would like to use all the authorized time to realize his original expectation.

Although Hong Kong was a colony of Great Britain, people still celebrated the Chinese New Year heartily. People wore their best new clothes. All the stores were closed. Firecrackers exploded one after another with deafening noise. Friends greeted each other with wishes of good fortune. Gambling marked another way of celebrating. Some people played Mahjongg on street sidewalks. The celebration did not have any meaning to Chang and Yeh. They were anxiously awaiting the result of Gimo's special trip to the United States.

A few days after the Lantern Festival (fifteenth day of the first lunar month), Gimo came to Hong Kong again. He told them about his trip to the United States to deliver their letters to Bob Ericson, who in turn contacted his former director of the U-2 project, Jim Cunningham, immediately. Jim had also retired from the CIA, but he knew who in the agency had the authority to render help. Two weeks after Gimo returned to Taiwan, he received a call from Bob and was asked him come to Hong Kong and take Chang and Yeh to an office in Hong Kong Island, where they would meet a United States official named Charlie.

Charlie told Chang and Yeh that he understood their intentions, but he had been ordered to conduct a thorough investigation. If both of them had no objection, he would like to talk with each one separately in another room. It was a lengthy interrogation followed by a polygraph test. The whole process lasted a whole afternoon. Both Chang and Yeh had nothing to hide. They did not have any problem going through the investigation. At the end of the investigation, Charlie told them:

"We are willing to help you. I hope you understand the delicate political situation. We are very reluctant to let the PRC know that we are helping you. I suggest you both move out of International House and stop communicating with everyone affiliated with the PRC, at least at this moment. If you agree, the Royal Hong Kong Yacht Club near here is a good place to stay."

Yeh said he would move to the Yacht Club. Chang said he would move to a friend's house on Hong Kong Island. Then Charlie handed each of them with three thousand dollars inside, and asked them to sign receipts. He gave them his telephone number just before they left his office. They did not ask for his last name, as from their experience in the Black Cat Squadron all the American colleagues were reluctant to let Chinese counterparts know their last names. Even when someone released his last name, was most likely an alias.

The American assistance stood in sharp contrast to the rejection of the ROC. Both Chang and Yeh were infuriated at the ungratefulness of the ROC government officials. They had fought Communist MiGs during the bombardment of Quemoy in 1958. They had

Lost Black Cats

risked their lives to penetrate the Bamboo Curtain many times to collect intelligence for the defense of ROC, and consequently had been captured by the enemy and suffered for many years under the Communist totalitarian regime. Even though they had practically stayed in the mainland longer than they had in Taiwan, they had never forgotten that they were the citizens of the Republic of China in Taiwan. How could the government refuse to let them return to their own country? When they were dispatched to undertake the U-2 missions, they were always told to collect intelligence for the Republic of China, not for the United States of America. Yet only the United States was willing to help them, and had offered the financial support at this critical moment.

The next morning, they got up very early. The weather was cooperative. A cold front had just passed over Hong Kong, which made the tropical climate drop to 40 ° F. They could now wear layers of clothes and put all the important documents in their pockets without showing any unusual appearance. They left all their belongings brought from the mainland intact in the room and walked out of the hotel in the twilight. The lobby was empty. A doorman greeted them:

"Good morning, sir. You are so early!"

"We like to enjoy the fresh air along the coast."

"Have a good day!"

They were happy that no one had noticed that they were leaving the International House for good. They caught the first ferryboat across Victoria Harbor. It was still too early to check into the Yacht Club or call the friend's home. They relaxed at a fast-food restaurant and then in a public park. They were fully aware this was a turning point of their lives. From now on, they would sever all the relations with the people in or from the mainland, at least temporarily.

The Club attendant seemed to have been informed in advance. He led Yeh to his room without any question. As for Charlie's advice that he should not let any secret agent of the PRC in Hong Kong find out where he was, Yeh started to live in self-imposed confinement. He rarely went outside of the club. He stayed most of the time in his room watching TV or reading newspaper. Sometimes he sat on a bench at the porch watching the airplanes taking off and landing at the Hong Kong airport on the other side of Kowloon Bay, and thinking that one of these days he would board one of those jumbo airliners to the United States.

He thought it would not be long before fulfilling his expectation. But a month passed and nothing happened. He called Charlie. Charlie told him that the U.S. government was negotiating with the government in Taiwan for ROC passports for both U-2 pilots. In this way, the United States could easily issue visas for them to enter the country. Otherwise, they might have to seek "political asylum" status, which would impose restrictions upon them, and the U.S. would possibly be blamed by the PRC for helping Yeh not to return to the mainland.

As the expiring date of their Hong Kong visas approached, Yeh called Charlie more often. No definite answer could be obtained, Yeh became increasingly uneasy. There was no assurance that the U.S. government would act for them, and it was not obliged to help him in the first place. If this were the case, he would be an illegal resident in Hong Kong until the Hong Kong police found and arrested him and deported him back to the mainland as a deserter.

Just one day before the Hong Kong visa expired, Charlie came to tell him that Yeh and Chang could leave for the United States on Pan American Airlines the following day.

Chapter Eleven: American Odyssey

On the morning of May 9, 1983, Chang came to join Yeh at the Yacht Club. Soon Charlie came to accompany them to the airport. The flight for Chang and Yeh to leave for the United States was scheduled for takeoff around two in the afternoon and the passengers were supposed to check in two hours before takeoff. So they had to leave the Yacht Club early enough. The Hong Kong airport was on the other side of the bay between the Hong Kong Island and Kowloon. They had to cross the bay by ferryboat and then reach the airport by taxi. Fortunately, they both had light luggage to carry.

After arriving at the airport, Charlie went into the Pan Am Airlines office for a while and then came out with tickets and boarding passes for the U-2 pilots. Then they went to a restaurant to have lunch. Charlie told them when the airplane landed in Los Angeles airport, a gentleman would come up to the airplane to receive them.

The Hong Kong airport was unique in its location. One side of the runway was the bay and the other side was facing the palisades of high-rise buildings. Yeh was assigned to a widow seat on the left. The multistoried buildings were very close to the runway. When the jumbo jet accelerated to airborne toward the open sea, he could see silhouettes moving inside the multistoried buildings, which made him remember the flights maneuvering on the deck when he was a RF-101 pilot.

Almost none of the photoreconnaissance aircraft carry weapons to defend themselves. They always maximize their special performance of evading enemy attack. Unlike the U-2 flying at an extraordinarily high altitude where no enemy fighter or anti-aircraft artillery could reach, RF-101 utilized its two jet engines with afterburners to accelerate itself swiftly to supersonic speed to escape from hostile pursuers. However, the mission of a photoreconnaissance aircraft was to take pictures of enemy targets. The targets were most likely armed with all sorts of anti-aircraft weapons: from small-caliber rifles to four-inch guns. They usually shot aimlessly to knit a fire net over the target to let the intruder hit the bullets by himself, if the enemy knew the reconnaissance aircraft was coming in advance. RF-101 pilots always flew as low as possible across the Taiwan Strait and over the mainland on the way to the target to avoid his intentions being detected by the enemy's early warning radar until reaching the target. Then he would pop up to an appropriate altitude for taking good pictures then leave the hot spot with full throttle.

The excitement and nervousness of controlling a high-speed aircraft flying a few inches above the treetops or the roofs, and hopping over a power line, had been buried in a corner of Yeh's memory for so many years. The scenery outside of the window made him remember the RF-101 missions he had carried out. He also remembered the feeling of gratification when he successfully completed a dangerous mission and flew the only aircraft in the blue sky heading home over the ocean where he could see both coast lines of the mainland and Taiwan, even though he knew that the reconnaissance pilot could never expect to become an instant celebrity like a fighter pilot who had shot down an enemy aircraft or destroyed an enemy target. Reconnaissance pilots should never tell anybody about what important intelligence he had collected in his mission except his supervisors. Otherwise, the enemy might get to know what their enemy had found out and they would change their deployment immediately. Nevertheless, Yeh knew that he had risked his life and made a valuable contribution to the defense of the Republic of China in Taiwan. This country would appreciate his contribution in the future. But the present situation was so inconceivable; it made Yeh feel sad, as the Republic of China did not welcome him returning home. He had to find a temporary dwelling place in a third country.

It was a twelve-hour non-stop direct flight over the Pacific Ocean across the International Date Line. They arrived in Los Angeles on the same day except four hours earlier. A gentleman wearing an orange jacket with a Black Cat emblem on his chest came forward to greet them as they just stepped out of the airplane to the boarding gate.

"Robin, Jack, do you still remember me? I used to be a security official in the Black Cat Squadron."

"Yes, I recognize you, but I don't remember your name. It seems that you have gained weight," Chang replied

"I am John Raines. We all grow more mature, don't we? Anyway, welcome to America!"

Chang's impression of John was that he was a young, humorous, and friendly American colleague in the squadron. Chang remembered the Chinese guards in the squadron sometimes called him "Big Nose" (大鼻子).

John led them through a special immigration booth. Then he accompanied them to board the Pan Am domestic flight to Washington, D.C., and told them there would be an agent to meet them at the destination.

The airplane arrived at the Washington Dulles Airport around six o'clock in the afternoon. They were very surprised to see that General Jim Cunningham had come to the airport to meet them in person. The other person they met at airport was Mr. Frank W___, who was still on active duty and responsible for taking care of them while they were staying in the United States. As the time went by, Frank finally became a close friend of theirs.

Frank took them to an apartment of the Parker House in Falls Church and told them U.S. government would pay the apartment rent and their living expenses until their status in the United States had been clarified. He would send another person to help them settle down tomorrow.

It was a furnished two-bedroom apartment. With all the modern appliances available, they needed almost nothing else to live a modest life, besides taking care of their own groceries and linens. They should be content to live here until their status had been clarified as Frank mentioned. But what kind of "status" did they have now? They asked Frank when they saw him the next time. Frank replied:

"Legally speaking, the ROC Air Force should treat you at least as ROC veterans, since you were officers of ROC Air Force when you executed the unfortunate missions; even though you had been captured by the enemy and harassed in mainland China for nearly twenty years. As long as you had not declared that you are willing to deny the ROC citizenship, you should still be ROC citizens, unless you have committed some unforgiving crime. We would like to have a consensus with your government before we can decide how we can support you. I was informed that the ROC Air Force would dispatch an officer to come to Washington to discuss this matter in the near future."

About two weeks later, Major General Lin Hsiche, Deputy Chief of Staff for Intelligence of the ROC Air Force came to Washington, D.C. He discussed this subject with U.S. government officials and talked with Chang and Yeh about their lives in the mainland, how they were released by the PRC, and their wishes for returning Taiwan in detail. He then said:

"I hope you understand the awkward situation our Air Force has right now. Before I left for this trip I went to seek guidance from General Wang Sheng, Executive Officer of the Political Department in the Ministry of National Defense, who is the most influential man in this subject matter area at this moment. He still insisted that we should not encourage military personnel to surrender instead of sacrificing their lives for their country. I don't think you can return to Taiwan soon. So I have negotiated with U.S. government officials and asked them to help you become permanent residents in the United States, and help you to find jobs. They agreed that they would appropriate a certain amount of money as pensions to support you for the rest of your lives. They asked that the Republic of China should support you accordingly. I estimate that the ROC can give you one hundred thousand dollars each, about half of which is back pay and the rest is pension. You know I have no power to authorize this appropriation. I have to submit my recommendation to a higher authority when I get back. It may take a quite a while to get approval."

Both of them were very upset by the word "surrender," for they were incapacitated at the time the Chinese Communists captured them. But there was no room for them to argue. The only way General Lin could help was to point out the misunderstanding of their actual situation in the mainland in his trip report submitted to his superiors when he returned to Taiwan. They added that if this case could be brought to President Chiang Chingkuo, they believed the problem would be solved right away, for President Chiang used to be the commanding official of the ROC and the U.S. U-2 joint operation. General Lin replied:

"You probably do not know what the political condition is now in Taiwan. President Chiang appointed Wang Sheng to lead a senior group (Liu Hsiaokang Office, 劉少康辦公室) to study and implement the strategy and tactics in countering the Chinese Communist Party's political offensive, since the United States severed diplomatic relations with the ROC in 1979. Ostensibly, the Communists advocate peaceful unification. Actually, they try by all means to isolate the ROC from the world community. Each time they normalize relations with a country, they always put the term 'Taiwan is a province of China' as an important condition. That practically caused most of the countries of the world to sever diplomatic relations with Taiwan. The aggressiveness of the Communist political offensive made the Liu Hsiaokang office expand its power continuously in the past several years to become 'a super cabinet within a cabinet.' President Chiang is now in bad health. He can hardly walk. Severe headaches frequently add to his suffering. People close to him generally think it is better not to bother him with minor decisions. Some senior officials even begin to suspect

Wang Sheng will take over the government after Chiang's death. I guess the Liu Hsiaokang office may regard your release from the mainland is a part of the Communist political offense. I don't think your case has the chance to reach President Chiang without going through Wang Sheng."

A few days later, Frank came to tell them:
"We have decided to help you obtain an immigration visa. However, our government has granted you political asylum. The law requires that you have to stay in the United States at least a year before applying for an immigration visa, which is generally called a "green card." You will be permitted to work after you receive the green card. In this case, we will support you living in this apartment until that time. In the meantime, we hope you will not let the PRC government know your situation. Please don't communicate with people in Communist China or anyone affiliated with them. On the other hand, you are free to communicate or visit your friends or relatives in the continental United States, or to communicate with someone in Taiwan."

Both of them had relatives living in the United States. Chang's daughter, Tsingyi, was now studying in graduate school at the University of Texas. Yeh was surprised to learn from his older brother, Yeh Chingyun, that all his siblings were living in North America. He had three brothers living in the United States, one in Las Vegas, one in St. Louis, and one in Buffalo. His sister was living in Los Angeles. He had another brother living in Vancouver, Canada. Besides relatives in the United States, Chang's beloved Chaichi and two sons were in Taiwan. Yeh's parents were still living in Taiwan.

Both of them spent much time reestablishing communication with their relatives. Yeh was anxious to let Betty and Hsiaotung know his new situation and to thank them for supporting him, both financially and spiritually, during the difficult time in Hong Kong. Much compassionate correspondence made them feel they were not alone anymore. It was the kind of feeling they had been deprived for so many years. Even though Yeh had married Xiaohung and been living with her for four months in the mainland, he could never say anything about his real thinking to her, without worrying his words might be recorded in the dossier to be used against him in a future wave of political struggle.

They also made the acquaintance of new friends in their nearby surroundings. Frank dispatched a Chinese-speaking employee, Mr. Chen, to help them in obtaining social security numbers and driver's licenses. Chen was very considerate in helping them start a normal life in this society. He often came to take them to the grocery store or to shopping malls. He even took them to tour the scenic spots in the D.C. area on weekends.

When the United States severed the diplomatic relations with the Republic of China in Taiwan in 1979, the ROC embassy was forced to change its name to the "Coordinate Council for North American Affairs (CCNAA)." All military attachés changed their titles to Chiefs of Service Coordination Offices. The Air Force Chief of Service Coordination Offices was Lin Wenli at that time. Chang and Yeh tried to keep in touch with Lin, for hopefully Lin would help them obtain permits to return to Taiwan in the future.

About three months later, Frank came to tell them that the CIA and its counterpart in the ROC had reached an agreement on how to support Chang and Yeh living in the United States. The CIA would provide two hundred thousand dollars and the ROC seventy five thousand dollars for each of them. The money would be invested in twenty-year treasury bonds. The interest of the bonds would be sufficient for them to live in the United States for the rest of their lives. Since the interest was paid semiannually, they each would be given twenty-five thousand dollars in cash to support them until the first interest was paid.

With the resources on hand, they bought cars and expanded the range of their activities. Chang traveled to Dallas, Texas, to visit his daughter, who came to the United States just three months ahead of Chang. It was a significant reunion between father and daughter. Tsingyi was only seven years old when Chang had been lost in the mainland. She had only vague impressions of what her father looked like; he assumed she would have changed completely, as most young girls do. Both of them appreciated that they were biologically related, yet each knew the other very little, like newly acquainted friends.

It was the year-end holiday season. Yeh's siblings organized a family reunion held in Las Vegas, where Yeh's older brother, Chingyun, resided. Chingyun was a classmate of Gimo Yang in the ROC Air Force academy. He worked for the ROCAF as a fighter pilot for many years. After he retired from the ROCAF as a major general, he immigrated to the United States a year ago. Yeh's sister was married to a classmate of Chingyun. The brother-in-law used to be a fighter pilot too. So three of them could speak the same language. Yeh's other three, younger brothers had all come to the United States and Canada to pursue higher education during the 1960s, and then stayed permanently in these countries. They all had happy families and established social status in their own fields.

A few days' reunion was a very busy one for Yeh. He had to get to know all the members of his extended family. He had to tell them his own miserable experience in Communist China. He was also interested in learning how his siblings had been doing in the past twenty years. One thing he had learned from their conversations was that the United States is a land of opportunity, even though racial discrimination caused some difficulties. He would be fifty-two years old when he became a permanent resident in the United States. Would he still have a chance to fulfill what is called the "American dream"?

When they acquired green cards in October 1984, Hsiaotung asked Yeh if he would join her to take over a fast-food restaurant in Houston. He accepted immediately. Hsiaotung and her husband were both working full-time for the Kellogg Oil Company in Houston. They were willing to invest their savings in the restaurant and would like to have Yeh be its manager.

At that time, Betty's husband had moved to teach at Princeton University in New Jersey. It was only three hours' drive from Washington, D.C. Yeh had been longing to see Betty since he arrived in the United States, yet one part of his mind warned him that both of them were married to other persons, and he should not make things complicated. He had debated with himself on this subject many times. Leaving the Washington, D.C., area to farther away soon might be a good reason to visit Betty. Yeh called Betty to inform her about his visit before assuming the job in Houston.

Betty was at home alone when Yeh arrived. Professor Huang and her two sons were still in school. Betty was more mature than he could remember. She made a cup of tea for him. She showed him her living environment and her family photos. As the conversation went on, Yeh felt there was something more than just friends between Betty and himself. They talked about many trivial events—some smart, some stupid, some they were proud of, some they were unhappy about—they had shared together more than twenty years ago. They also talked about the miserable time they both had had after Yeh's catastrophic mission. Yeh almost told her about his attempted suicide after being informed of the bad news of Betty's remarriage, yet his conscience told him that he had no right to make her feel bad.

Professor Huang came back for lunch. He treated him cordially. Yet Yeh subconsciously sensed there was uneasiness among three of them. He found an excuse to leave for Washington, D.C., after the lunch.

Being manager of a fast-food restaurant is a twenty-four-hour seven-day-a-week job. It was a new challenge to Yeh. Fortunately, he had sufficient English background and did not take long to manage the business fully under his control. He started to have time to think about Xiaohung. Even though the marriage had been arranged by the Communist Party, they had only stayed together for four months, and she had carried someone else's baby, Yeh thought he still had unfinished business in mainland China. He wrote a letter to her to tell her he was sorry he had not been able to write to her sooner due to the complicated situation. He did not tell her what kind of complications. He only told her that he was now a manager of a restaurant in the United States and was anxious to know how she was doing.

About twenty days later, Xiaohung's letter arrived. In that letter she wrote,

"… After several weeks of not receiving your letter, I went to ask Cadre Xu to see whether he could find out what happened to you. He later told me that you and Chang both disappeared in Hong Kong since the Chinese New Year. I waited and waited until your Hong Kong Visa expired. I knew that you would never come back again. My father told me it was better to file for divorce. So I did…. I went back to work for the same textile mill when the school told me that they would not let me have your salary…. A few months ago, my old boss told me he had divorced his wife. We are now married…. I have still kept your belongings. If you like I can mail them to you…."

Yeh did not have any interest in remembering any of his nineteen-year wretched life. There was no sense in having those belongings back. He wrote back to her,

"… I am very happy to know that you two in love can finally live together. Thank you for keeping my belongings. Please don't bother to mail them to me, just dispose of them at your convenience…."

Xiaohung did not mention whether she had had an abortion or whether the baby was a boy or girl. It was not Yeh's business anymore. The letters brought an episode of Yeh's pathetic life to its closure. He felt like he had released a burden.

The fast-food restaurant was closed on the afternoon of New Year's Eve. Yeh was invited to have dinner at Hsiaotung's home. After the dinner they relaxed in the living room to enjoy a Jasmine tea. Hsiaotung told Yeh:

"There is something I have not told you. Not long after you came to Houston, Betty's husband called me. He told me that your presence made their marriage vulnerable, since you and Betty had never been officially divorced. He hoped I could convince you to go through some kind of legal process to declare you and Betty are legally separated. I thought it was not practical at all, for you might be required to go back to Taiwan to do that and you could not go to Taiwan for the time being. You know what? Just a few days ago, he called me again and said, 'Hsiaotung, forget about what I asked you. My brother-in-law had helped me acquire a copy of the ROC Air Force official document declaring Yeh had died in line of duty.' I didn't know professor Huang is so serious about this."

It surprised Yeh too. He tried to think what made Professor Huang take it so seriously. Had Yeh and Betty had some kind of gesture during Yeh's visit to them before he came to Houston, which caused Professor Huang to have so much concern? Anyway, Huang must value his family life as most important to him, and did not wish to be interfered with by any intruder. Conscientiously, Yeh should not disturb someone's peaceful life. He decided to refrain from contacting Betty from that time on, even though he still loved Betty so much.

Chang found a job as a security guard in a retirement community in McLean. The residents of this community were all military veterans. To a person like Chang, with the military background, it was a nice environment to work with. People in the community were friendly. An ex-fighter pilot could still win some respect.

The community provided Chang with a studio apartment. He decorated his apartment with pictures of aircraft, which he had collected in the past year. He was still longing to fly fighters, even though he knew he would never have a chance to fly again. On his desk there were the pictures of his daughter and sons. No matter when he would be able to reunite with Chaichi, who was now married to another man, Chingli will always be his daughter, Tsingyi and Luke his sons.

The security guards worked in three shifts. Chang started working on the graveyard shift, which had a smaller workload and less involvement with people. The job as security guard led him to live a well-regulated life, for which Chang had been trained since middle-school age. He thought this was a good way to wait until the requirement of "living in the third country for five years" was fulfilled, before applying for a permit for returning Taiwan.

The climate was hot and humid in Houston during the summer. The temperature did not come down much in late fall. A hurricane came from Gulf of Mexico to quench the heat. The strong winds left the falling leaves and branches of trees strewn around. The heavy rain brought dirt and garbage to the front of the fast-food restaurant. Yeh spent quite an effort to clean them, in addition to the routine work of managing the restaurant. He was very exhausted. The remaining missile fragments in his thighs and legs bothered him again. For many years, those fragments always caused aching when the humidity was high, but not as severe as this time.

He finally sat down and said to himself, "Why do I have to bear such a heavy workload? I am not young and healthy anymore." He had managed the restaurant almost a year. His hard work rewarded him a handsome amount of profit. But what was useful to him with that money? He had no one who depended on his support. He had no one who would be pleased with his money. He even did not have time to spend that money himself. He decided to convince Hsiaotung to put the restaurant back on the market for sale again.

A few days after the new year of 1986, the restaurant was taken over by a new owner. Yeh was happy to have free time to relax. Then a friend, the owner of the Park Avenue Jewelry Store, asked him to help him in managing his store. He started to learn the trade of jewelry business.

Yeh's mother wrote him that his father was very sick and hoped to see him again in Taiwan. He went to the liaison office of CCNAA in Houston to apply for the permit to Taiwan. The clerk said to him:

"Do you have an ROC passport? If so, you don't have to apply for visa."

"I don't have one."

"Do you have an American passport?"

"No. I only have a U.S. driver's license and a green card."
The clerk refused to accept the application form.

Two weeks later, his mother called him by phone to tell him his father had reached terminal stage and asked him to rush back. He immediately called the Air Force Chief of the Service Coordination Office, CCNAA, in Washington, D.C., for help. He went to the Taiwan Liaison Office next day. The clerk still refused to accept his application. Then he requested to see her supervisor. A gentleman came out the back office and said:

"Mr. Yeh, CCNAA had told me your case. I fully understand your situation. But I have no power to issue the permit to you. I will report this case to the Ministry of Foreign Affairs in Taiwan."

"How soon can I expect their response?"

"Maybe in a few days."

"Could you call me when the permission arrives?"

"No problem."

Yeh put down his telephone number and left. The call did not come for quite some time. Yeh went back to the liaison office many times in the following days. The answers were always, "Pending." When Yeh's father died, and the memorial service was held, there was still no instruction delivered to the liaison office. Then Yeh's siblings decided to move their mother to live with their sister in Los Angeles. Yeh had no need to find out what happened to his request anymore.

Chang's daughter, Tsingyi, completed her graduate education. She was ready to get married in the summer of 1986. The bride's father traveled to Dallas to give away his daughter to a nice-looking young accountant. Chaichi came to Dallas too.

After the wedding ceremony and reception, the newlyweds had a honeymoon at a nearby resort. Chang had more time to be with Chaichi alone than Chaichi's last trip to visit her daughter a year before. They had more time to talk about how they had been doing recently. He learned more about how Chaichi's mother persuaded her to marry Ho. Ho was already retired from the army and worked for the Executive Yuan as an administrator at that time. He is fourteen years older than Chaichi. He had been single for more than twenty-six years since the war between the KMT and the CCP, which made Ho lose contact with his wife of three months' marriage. There was no hope for him to reunite with his wife in the mainland under the current political situation. The age and the relaxed workload made him feel like having a family. He really wanted Chaichi to be his companion for life and treated her three children as his own.

As for Chang, no matter how nice Ho was, he was anxious to reunite with Chaichi. He asked:

"Chaichi, I have settled down now. I have a secure job. My income is sufficient for us to have decent lives in the United States. When do you think you can leave Ho and come to me?"

She responded, "I know you have waited for so long. But I hope you understand that the situation is not so simple. In the past twelve years Ho devoted all his efforts to this family. He helped me take care of my bedridden father and then my sick mother until the days they died and were buried. He helped me raise all three children. I just cannot simply ask him for a divorce because of you. You know, not long after your sudden appearance in Hong Kong, he said to me, 'I know you love Liyi more. Please don't kick me out of this family. I am sixty-two years old. I have nowhere to go. Just let me stay and treat me as an old butler.' It sounded so pathetic. He has no relatives in Taiwan. I had borne three children for you. Yet I did nothing for him."

"You said he had a wife in the mainland. Why did he not go back to his old wife? I met someone from Taiwan in Hong Kong who was returning from a trip to the mainland. You can encourage him to go to the mainland. Maybe he can find a son or daughter there too."

"The government is still forbidding all government employees and veterans to visit the mainland. I believe when you are allowed to come back to Taiwan, he will fulfill his promise and leave."

A moment later, Chaichi added:

"The culture around here is so different from what we have in Taiwan. I don't know if I ever were able to get used to living in this environment. If I came to the United States, I would have to give up my job. I have been working in the same office for more than twenty years. Seniority means respect and privilege. I like my job very much. If I come here, I have to leave all my good friends there too. So for the time being, let us wait for the day when you come back to Taiwan."

It seemed to Chang there was no room for argument. Chang accompanied her to tour some scenic spots around Dallas and then saw her off at the airport. A month later, Tsingyi and her husband move to New York City. She started to work for the Bank of New York. New York is much closer to Washington than Dallas. So Chang could go to see them occasionally.

Another year passed, Chaichi came to New York to visit her daughter and son-in-law. This time her elder son, Chingyi, came along with her. Chang drove to New York to meet them. It was almost a family reunion, except that Luke, their younger son, was still in Taiwan. He was not permitted to go abroad before he had finished his compulsory military service.

Chang found a time to talk with Chaichi.

"I heard that the government had relaxed its control of the veterans' and government employees' travel to the mainland. Did Ho go to the mainland?"

"He did. You know what he told me after his visit? He said, 'I will never go back to the mainland again. My previous wife and relatives thought I was going back to repay my debts to them. The Communists treated them badly, even tortured them, only because I worked for the KMT. It was the fault of the Communists. Yet they expected me to compensate their loss.'"

"What should we do now?"

"Don't worry. I found out just recently he is looking for some government-provided facilities for old veterans, although he did not tell me why."

The reunion was the highlight of Chang's quiet life. Although it was only a week together, Chang felt like he had reunited with his family.

In January of 1988, the news of President Chiang's death came to the United States. Both Chang and Yeh were sad, for now their cases would never be rectified. The U-2 program was top secret when Yeh and Chang were in the Black Cat Squadron. Not many people, not even Commander-in-Chief of the ROC Air Force, knew the detailed operations. President Chiang was the only one of the few officials who knew this secret project and was still in a powerful position of the government. As the president passed away, who would speak for them anymore?

This condition worried Chang even more, for he was looking forward to the day when he would be permitted to return to Taiwan. The "living in the third country for five years before applying for entry permit" requirement was almost met now. What impact would the recent political environment have on his application? From the experience Yeh had in dealing with the Houston Liaison Office, he had better contact the Air Force Chief of the Service Coordination Office, CCNAA, first to find out what kind of attitude the government had toward his case. It was probably because the government was still in the stage of growing pains following President Chiang's initiation on the political reform to transform the country into a democratic model of China, and also both the military threat and the political offensiveness of the Chinese Communists continuously posted on the other side of the Taiwan Strait, that no one at the high level paid much attention to Chang's request. No definite response was received from Taiwan. Chang might have to wait for a long time.

It was not so serious for Yeh, since he did not have any need to go back to Taiwan. He was intrigued with the tricks of the jewelry trade. Thoughtful friends sometimes introduced single ladies to him, as they thought Yeh should have a family. He was fifty-five years old and had sound financial foundation. However, there was only a small Chinese community in the Houston area, and Yeh did not believe happy marriage could exist across cultural differences. He did not find anyone he liked until he met Keiko in late 1988.

Keiko was fourteen years younger than Yeh, yet mature enough to be good company. In the beginning Yeh was hesitant to get deeply involved partially due to his unhappy experience with his previous two short marriages. As the time went by and they got to know each other more, Yeh gradually found a new meaning of his life.

Chapter Twelve: Rehabilitation

It was the year-end holiday season of 1988. Yeh went to Los Angeles, where his mother lived with his sister, to participate in another family reunion. He also took this opportunity to visit many of his friends in that area, including some retired ROC Air Force colleagues and John Raines, the agent who met him at the gate when he arrived in the United States by plane from Hong Kong five and a half years ago. One evening, a gentleman with an English accent phoned Yeh and introduced himself as a writer in the process of publishing a book on U-2 operations. He said:

"Mr. Yeh, this is Chris Pocock from England. I have a friend who used to work for the CIA. He told me your unique story of U-2 missions and later being captured and confined in Communist China for nineteen years. He gave me your telephone number and recommended that I contact you. I think your miserable experience should be made known to the public. Could we get together sometime tomorrow to have a talk?"

It was an offer Yeh could hardly refuse, as the stuffy feeling of having received a cold shoulder from the Taiwan government needed venting. He accepted having an interview. They had a lengthy talk in a coffee shop. Then Chris said:

"I am on the way back to London. I will stop over in Washington, D.C. My friend gave me Chang's address and phone number. It appears to me he is living somewhere near D.C. I may find time to interview him too, if he has no objection."

"I think he would like to talk to you. When the book is published would you mail me a copy?"

"I certainly will do that."

Chris came to see Chang along with another American friend. Chang invited them to have a Chinese dinner. Their friendly conversation provided Chris with sufficient information he needed to write his book.

The book with the title *Dragon Lady* was published by Airlife Publishing Ltd. in England in April 1989. The book allocated about twenty pages to a depiction of the ROC and U.S. joint operation over China and its vicinities. It also included an epilogue describing several events indirectly related to the U-2 operations. The unfair treatment Yeh and Chang had received from the ROC government, and how they moved to the United States, were also briefly described as the first event in that section.

The book soon became popular, as the secret nature of the U-2 operations itself was an interesting subject to read, not only in the intelligence community, but also to the people who had heard the dramatic episode of the Gary Powers incident. It was unfortunate that the book did not attract much attention in Taiwan, as it was written in English. Not many people there could appreciate the writing until the beginning of 1990, when a reporter from the Taiwanese *United Daily News*, Peng Kuangyang, stationed in the United States, found this book and introduced it to a colleague in Taiwan, Ong Taisheng, who translated the part related to the Taiwan operation in *Dragon Lady* into Chinese and published sequentially in the *United Daily News* (聯合報). Peng and another reporter also interviewed Chang and Yeh and published two articles in the *Chinese World Weekly* (世界周刊) in the United States. The Chinese public, both in Taiwan and in the United States, gradually realized the situation Chang and Yeh had endured.

Consequently, the ROC Air Force ordered the Air Force Chief of the Service Coordination Office, CCNAA, to notify them that they could apply for the permit now. But to Chang and Yeh, it was not a complete answer. The message did not mention how the government would treat them when they returned to Taiwan.

At the funeral of Yeh's mother held in Los Angeles in February 1990, one reporter asked Yeh for his opinion. He answered:

"I can never understand why we had to endure such unjust punishment. Am I still a major of the ROC Air Force? If not, what crime have I committed for them to dismiss me from the service? Did they ever consider I was well decorated for many dangerous missions?

"Am I still a citizen of the Republic of China? They have no reason to deny my citizenship. Why can I not have an ROC passport?

"Each time I have read a report or watched a TV broadcast on how the United States ceremoniously welcomed the American prisoners of war released by enemies, even the POWs who had been coerced into denouncing their own country, I could hardly calm myself down for many days. I just don't understand why my government could not do the same."

In April, Ong, with the cooperation of Pocock, published a book about the Chinese part of the U-2 operation in Chinese titled *Black Cat Squadron* (黑貓中隊) in Taiwan. The book reprinted the articles published in the *Chinese World Weekly* and stirred up quite a lot of sympathetic public comment toward Chang and Yeh. In a public hearing conducted in the Legislative Yuan (立法院, equivalent to the Congress in the United States), Legislator Chao Shaokang questioned Minister of National Defense Hau Pochun about the case of the two U-2 pilots. Minister Hau replied that the Ministry of National Defense was in the process of welcoming them home to Taiwan.

Not long after that hearing, ROC passports for Chang and Yeh were issued by CCNAA and airline tickets from China Airlines were mailed to them. At that time Yeh had already become engaged to Keiko. Keiko's parents were living in Taiwan. It was a good opportunity for Yeh to meet his in-laws-to-be. Keiko planned to arrive in Taiwan five days later than Yeh, to avoid getting involved in some official ceremonies for Chang and Yeh.

The flight was scheduled to leave Los Angeles on the afternoon of September 3.

They both arrived in Los Angeles a day before departure. Many retired ROC colleagues residing in that area organized a warm farewell party that evening and saw them off at the airport the following day. When they stepped on a Boeing 747 of China Airlines, an airline attendant led them to the first-class seats. Chang said:

"Miss, we don't have first-class tickets. Are you making a mistake?"

"No, sir. Captain told us to upgrade your seats to first class."

While the airplane was still on the ground, to Chang's surprise, his son, Chingyi showed up.

"Father, I am the Chief cabin attendant of this airplane. Yesterday, after our airlines found out you would be on this flight, they dispatched me to take this duty."

"I never thought I would meet you here. Chingyi, come meet your uncle Yeh. By the way, who is the captain of the flight?"

"Fan Hungti. I was told he was also a U-2 pilot."

Both of them did not know Fan, for he had joined the Black Cat Squadron much later than they did. After a short moment of conversation, Chingyi went back to continue his duties.

The airplane took off on time and climbed up to the cruising altitude. Weather is always good on top of the clouds. The first-class cabin was only half filled. Passengers started to move around, or stretched their legs by lying on the almost flattened reclining seats, and enjoyed delicious hors d'oeuvres and cocktails. The captain came out of the cockpit and greeted them.

"Instructors (兩位教官, the respectful address commonly used by junior pilot to call the senior pilots in the ROC Air Force), I am very glad to have the chance to serve you on this flight."

"Thank you for upgrading our seats."

"You probably have never heard my name. I reported to the Black Cat Squadron about two years after you had left the squadron. I had my first mission over the mainland in March 1967. You know the penetration missions stopped in 1968. I was fortunate to have had the chance of carrying out the last mission over the mainland."

"How do you like being a captain of a Boeing 747?"

"It is much easier to fly this jumbo jet than handling a U-2. It really needs skill to fly a U-2. But the captain of an international airline has more responsibility."

Fan sat down on a nearby seat. They chatted about their mutual acquaintances. They talked about how the old Black Cat colleagues were doing. Fan went back to the cockpit when the stewardess started to serve dinner.

It was a thirteen-hour non-stop flight. With the special attention of Chang's son and the warm service of stewardesses, they were practically the VIPs on this flight. After two meals plus a snack and two movies, the airplane landed in Chiang Kaishek International Airport in Taiwan around eight o'clock in the evening of September 4, 1990.

When they stepped out of the airplane, an Air Force captain saluted them and introduced himself as an assigned escort. He told his subordinate to take both U-2 pilots' passports to complete the immigration and custom formalities, and led them through a different passage to the reception hall. Many of their old colleagues and friends were already waiting there to welcome them. Someone came forward to put garlands around their necks. Among the crowds, to Chang's surprise, came Chiachi, who gave Chang a nosegay. In the Chinese tradition, a gentleman is not supposed to hug a lady in public; hence, Chang held her hands for a long time. He was so excited and could hardly help from crying in the midst of welcomers and reporters. He wanted to say something, but no words came out of his mouth. Longing for so many years, this should be the end.

All the welcomers wanted to shake hands with them. Many of the welcomers said they were sorry that the government had not treated them fairly. After having left Taiwan for more than a quarter of a century, it was difficult for Yeh and Chang to recognize most of the welcomers.

The escort captain took them to the Air Force Activities Center by sedan and led them to the reserved rooms. He told them that the room and board would be taken care by the Air Force as long as they were staying there. He said if they did not have any other plans, he would come to take them to see General Lin Wenli, Commander-in-Chief of the Air Force, at nine o'clock tomorrow morning in his office.

General Lin was the Air Force Chief of the Service Coordination Office, CCNAA at Washington, D.C., when Chang and Yeh arrived there in 1983. General Lin knew their situation very well. When they came into his office he said to them:

"Liyi, Changti, I am so glad your wishes have finally materialized."

"Commander-in-Chief, we are here to report ourselves to the Air Force."

"I appreciate very much your wish of working for the Air Force. However, according to the military regulations, majors should be retired after twenty years' service. In other words, if an Air Force major was commissioned to be an officer at age twenty-two, he has to be retired at age forty two. I think you both exceed the age limit."

"But we have never been formally discharged."

"I have considered this problem already. Tomorrow morning we will have a formal ceremony at the headquarters for your honorable discharge. Tonight I have invited many of your colleagues to have a dinner party in the Air Force Activities Center to welcome your return to Taiwan."

There were about thirty-some people attending that welcoming dinner party. Besides several high-ranking Air Force officers and many old members of the Black Cat Squadron, many classmates of Chang and Yeh were also invited. The reminiscences of Chang and Yeh's lives in the past three decades were certainly the main subjects of conversation.

As an ex-U-2 pilot of the Black Cat Squadron, the author of this book was also invited to participate in this dinner party. He had a chance to talk with Yeh.

"Do you still remember me, Robin?"

"Certainly, you and I shared the same room when we were working for the Black Cat Squadron. I remember you were reading books all the time. I admired you, for you could concentrate on studying something in that environment while the shadow of dangerous missions was frequently cast over you."

"We all have interesting lives, don't we?"

From the story Chang and Yeh revealed at this dinner party, the author made up his mind that if the opportunity arose, he would write a book on their miserable experience.

The honorable discharge ceremony was cordial. General Lin praised their sacrifices and contributions to the country and then pinned medals on the chests of both returning Black Cats. The following reception tea party let Chang and Yeh meet many other Air Force officers. One of the officers was the director of the Political Department of the ROC Air Force, Lieutenant General Hsu Mingtang, who was Yeh's classmate in the Air Force Academy. They talked about what Yeh intended to do after the ceremony. Yeh told him that his fiancé would come to Taiwan the day after tomorrow and he planned to meet her parents.

"Are you going to get married soon?" Lieutenant General Hsu asked.

"Most likely. You know, this will be the first time I will have met her parents."

"Are you planning to marry in Taiwan?"

"We did consider it this way."

"If so, the Air Force will manage the wedding ceremony for you."

"We don't want to bother too many people, for this is not the first wedding for either of us."

"I think it is very different from the previous ones. Don't you feel like being 'born again' now?"

"But my financial condition does not allow me to have a luxury wedding."

"Don't worry. The Air Force will take care of the expenses."

Yeh looked at the shining stars on Hsu's blue epaulets and remembered Hsu was not an outstanding alumnus of his class when he was already a well-decorated reconnaissance pilot. But now Hsu had become a Lieutenant General of the ROC Air Force. He was just a retired Major. He dejectedly realized that for his unfortunate overflight mission he had wasted all the twenty-seven years, those most productive years of human life!

That afternoon and the following day, the assigned escort accompanied them to tour the various principal places of interest in Taipei City and its vicinities, such as the memorials of Dr. Sun Yatsen and Generalissimo Chiang Kaishek, the Palace Museum, etc. After so many years away, Taipei had become almost a strange place to them. The high-rises along the widened roads changed the whole perspective of the city completely from what they could remember. Automobiles and motorcycles competed with each other for the right of the way. Everybody seemed to have plenty of money to spend. They were told the superhighway had shortened the distance across the island. It only took half the time as before to reach the southern part of Taiwan by automobile now. There also were regional airlines flying between cities hourly. The economic boom had made so many differences.

At their request, the escort took them to visit the tombs that the Air Force had built for them in the Pitan cemetery. The caretaker showed them the site of their tombs and told them the tombstones had been taken away right after the Communists announced their release. So far those plots had not been assigned to other martyrs.

They teased each other and said the plots were reserved as final resting places for them.

On a Saturday afternoon in late September, the auditorium of the Air Force Activity Center was crowded again. Many dignitaries of the armed services had shown up, among two hundred some guests. It was the wedding ceremony of Yeh and Keiko. The red congratulatory silk scrolls pinned with blessing golden characters decorated the walls. A pair of big red candles was lit on the podium. The most senior veteran of ROC Armed Forces, General Wang "Tiger" Shuming, was the witness of the marriage standing behind the podium. General Lin acted as the bridegroom's father, standing on one side of the witness. Keiko's father stood on the other side of the witness. During the music of "The Wedding March," the bride and groom walked slowly down the middle aisle between the guests and stopped in front of the podium facing the witness. After a long string of firecrackers exploded outside of the auditorium, the witness made a pleasant, short speech. Then he stamped his seal on a pair of wedding certificates laid on the podium. Both General Lin and Keiko's father, following the witness, stamped their seals on the certificates. The bride and groom exchanged the wedding rings to the applause of the guests. Someone stood up and asked loudly for the newlyweds kiss each other in public.

An extravagant banquet was the reception of the wedding ceremony. The guests came to congratulate the newlyweds along with toasts. Many of them recommended both the bride and the groom to have a "bottoms up" together. Yeh always refused politely by saying, "Thank you for your friendly motive. But we have already bought the airline tickets to leave tomorrow in the early morning for Hawaii to have our honeymoon there."

Yeh's Family reunion at Los Angeles 1987

Chang could not help but cry when he received a nosegay from Chaichi in the midst of welcome crowd.
Taipei International Airport, September 4, 1990.

Chang's Family 1991

Chang and Chaichi reaffirm their wedding vows.

ROC U-2 pilots and wives participated Recon Rendezvous 2003 at Air Force Museum, Dayton, Ohio.
From left to right: the author, Margaret Hua, Gimo Yang, Keiko Yeh, Robin Yeh, and Johnny Shen.

Epilogue

Chang quit his job in McLean, Virginia, and returned to Taiwan to reunite with Chaichi, his two sons, and their families. Chaichi continued to work for China Airlines until 1995. Living in a warm family made Chang sometimes think about the lonely life being led by Ho Chungtsun, who reluctantly had left Chaichi for Chang's return and had been living in a military retirement community in southern Taiwan. He was over eighty years old. Chang would like to meet him and thank him for taking care of his wife and children for so many years. But Ho refused to see him. However, Chingyi and Luke, both Chang's sons, visited Ho occasionally.

After Chaichi retired from China Airlines, Chang and Chaichi took a tour of mainland China. Chang found that living standards in the mainland had improved significantly in the past fifteen years. They visited Chang's siblings and Chaichi's distant relatives in Nanjing. They went to Beijing to call on Kuo Di, the cadre who had overseen Chang and Yeh's lives while they were on the mainland. Kuo had retired too, yet he told one of his subordinates to arrange a dinner party for Chang and his wife in the same private room of the Noble Court of the Beijing Hotel where they had had dinner in 1982. Several cadres who had supervised Chang from time to time were invited too, although Kuo could not show up himself as he was sick and in hospital.

While Chang and Chaichi were visiting their daughter and their granddaughter in New York in the summer of 2002, as they routinely did in the summer every year while the weather in Taiwan is so steamy, she was diagnosed as having a hereditary kidney decease, which could not be cured by any available medical treatment. They returned to Taiwan and her health deteriorated continuously until the day she died in August 2003.

Yeh returned to Houston and worked for the Park Avenue Jewelry Store as one of its managers until 1998. As age showed up among his siblings, and the extended family continuously expanded, his family reunions had to be held less frequently. They tried to keep the reunion to at least once every two years. Yeh and Keiko visited Taiwan many times, since Keiko's parents were still living there.

After Yeh's retirement, the couple joined an American tour group to visit mainland China. The guided tour did give him different perspectives on those places he had been before. He also recognized the changes in both the cities and the countryside. Probably because they were using American passports, none of Yeh's old acquaintances on the mainland noticed they were visiting. They did not meet any of them.

The first gathering of USAF Cold War Reconnaissance Organizations, "Recon Rendezvous 2003," was held in the United States Air Force Museum near Dayton, Ohio, September 3-6, 2003. Several survived Chinese U-2 pilots, with their spouses living in the United States and Canada, were invited to participate. The gathering included a day-long reconnaissance symposium held in the Air Force theater chaired by Mr. Cargill Hall, the Chief Historian for the National Reconnaissance Organization, on the fifth of September. The author was asked to give a PowerPoint presentation on the ROC-US joint U-2 operations over China and its vicinities. The author described on one of the missions how the Chinese Communists had deployed four SA-2 surface-to-air missile battalions to form a front of SA-2s, positioned at about twenty-five-mile intervals, in an attempt to ambush Yeh's U-2 and foil his maneuver of evasion. The first missile missed him but the second one brought him down. The author said:

"… The pilot of that mission was Major Yeh, who was severely wounded and lost consciousness upon reaching the ground. Then he was captured by the Chinese Communists and released nineteen years later. We are fortunate to have Major Yeh and his wife, Keiko, here today. Major Yeh, please stand up."

The audience responded with a long applause to show their respect.

In a recent conversation, Yeh told the author:

"By God's grace, I finally found a loving and caring companion for my golden years. Time has passed so fast. We have now been living together for almost fourteen years. I am so grateful."

Printed in the United States
29669LVS00005B/183